Just A Cotton Field

By Debra Hughey

The Scuppernong Press

Wake Forest, NC

www.scuppernongpress.com

Just A Cotton Field

©2018 Debra Hughey

First Printing

The Scuppernong Press
PO Box 1724
Wake Forest, NC 27588
www.scuppernongpress.com

Cover painting by Bill Weaver

Cover and book design by Frank B. Powell, III

All rights reserved. Printed in the United States of America.

No part of this book may be reproduced or transmitted in any form or by any means, electronic or mechanical, including photocopying, recording, or by any information and storage and retrieval system, without written permission from the editor and/or publisher.

International Standard Book Number ISBN 978-1-942806-18-9

Library of Congress Control Number: 2018955374

Table of Contents

Forward 1
Acknowledgements 3
Chapter 1 Fishing Trip 5

Part One — Seasons of Change

Chapter 2 The Horseshoe Revisited 9
Chapter 3 Hillabee Home 13
Chapter 4 Wagon Full of Children 19
Chapter 5 Eyes for No Other 23
Chapter 6 Fox Slayer 27
Chapter 7 Secrets to Share 31
Chapter 8 Green Corn Once Again 35
Chapter 9 Time of the Cold Moon 39
Chapter 10 1825 — Time of New Leaves 45
Chapter 11 Home, Sweet Home 49
Chapter 12 Down the Tallapoosa 53
Chapter 13 Tuckabatchee Council 57
Chapter 14 Eyes That See Me 63
Chapter 15 Instructions for the Law Menders 67
Chapter 16 Penalty of Death 71
Chapter 17 The Deed Is Done 75
Chapter 18 Return to the Tallapoosa 79

Part Two — Hard Times to Come

Chapter 19 Owl of Wood 85

Chapter 20 Grave Words from Sharp Knife 89

Chapter 21 Wisdom of a Child 93

Chapter 22 Word from Opothle Yahola 97

Chapter 23 Little Dove 103

Chapter 24 We Will Eat and Dance 107

Chapter 25 We Will Not Go 111

Chapter 26 Surveyors on Creek Land 115

Chapter 27 This is Our Home 119

Chapter 28 We Are Hungry 121

Chapter 29 We Are Too Old to Fight 125

Chapter 30 Her Bones Will Lie Here 127

Chapter 31 Red Streaked Stone 131

Chapter 32 Be Strong 135

Chapter 33 Snap of a Whip 139

Chapter 34 The Holding Pen 143

Chapter 35 Time to Go 147

Chapter 36 I Feel It 153

Epilogue 159

Foreword

Just A Cotton Field is the third in a series of the story of the Hillabee Chieftain Soaring Eagle and his family. *The Owl and the Horseshoe* tells of the family in the time before the big battle at the Horseshoe and how they dealt with the horrors of that day.

Spirit of the Red Stick Women continues the story after the power of the mighty Creek Nation was broken and how the spirit of the grandmothers provided the strength for survival for Soaring Eagle and the Hillabee people.

The great influx of white settlers continued to change the lives of the Creek people and was even a threat to their existence. *Just A Cotton Field* is the story of the tremendous hardship and struggle in the years prior to the removal of the Creek people.

All three books are based on actual historical events that happened during the real-life saga of the native people. Soaring Eagle and his family are, of course, fictitious characters. It is my hope that these people become real to you, just as they have to me. Come, let us go back in time now to the spring of 1819 and see what *Just A Cotton Field* meant to the people who lived along the Tallapoosa.

Acknowledgements

Books

A Historical Analysis of the Creek Indian Hillabee Towns,
Don C. East

The Triumph of The Ecunnau-Nuxulgee
William W. Winn

Creek Indian Medicine Ways, The Enduring Power of Muskokee Religion
David Lewis, Jr., and Ann T. Jordan

Maps and Photos

Indians of North America, The Creeks
Michael D. Green, Frank W. Porter III, General Editor
Map of Upper and Lower Creek Towns

Maptech Terrain Navigator 2002 Topography Map

White Oak Creek (Harbuck), Pinchneyville, Clay County, Alabama

McIntosh Reserve, Whitesburg, Georgia

Pole Cat Springs, Moore-Davis Nursery, Shorter, Alabama

Just A Cotton Field Photo, Site of Tuckabatchee, Taylor Farms, Tallassee, Alabama

Gone But Not Forgotten, Painting by Bill Weaver

Home Sweet Home Lyrics written by John Howard Payne

Personal Acknowledgements

Thanks to Jeanna Kervin for Editing Assistance

And

A Special Thanks to My Husband, Fred Randall Hughey, who has contributed many hours to make *Just A Cotton Field* a reality.

Chapter One
Fishing Trip, August 2017

The morning sun had not yet appeared over the eastern bank of the Tallapoosa as the young man maneuvered his old beat up truck off the main highway onto the narrow dirt road. His slightly newer bass boat bouncing, fishing rods sliding from one side of the boat to the other as he tried in vain to miss the dried up mudholes that stretched across the little road. The young man laughed as his friend grabbed the door handle in an effort to balance himself. He had promised him an easy, peaceful day of fishing on the lower Tallapoosa River and so far, they had gotten off to a rough, bumpy start and they were later than he had hoped. He wanted to get to the river before the sunlight filtered through the Spanish moss that hung from the old oak trees and while the mist and fog still floated over the water. Fishing would be best then, but he loved that time on the river. The brief time before the gray dawn gave way to the new day. Matthew Walker smiled again as his buddy, Jacob East held on tightly with one hand and tried to keep his cap on his head with the other.

"Hey man, I thought you said we were going to have an easy, peaceful day down here," Jacob said as the truck tire again dipped into an even deeper rut, causing the heads of both young men to bump the top of the truck.

"Sorry 'bout that," Matthew said, laughing, "I guess I really should slow down. I just wanted to get down to the river before the sun comes up."

"Why is that so important, the fish aren't going anywhere are they," Jacob asked as he looked for the button to open the window. "How do you let this thing down, anyway?"

Matthew looked at Jacob in disbelief. "With the handle, ugh, you just turn it. I don't reckon you've ridden in old trucks too much. Ah, you do know how to fish don't you?" Matthew asked as he rolled his own window down. He was beginning to wonder if his "city-boy" friend had ever been to the country before, much less felt the excitement of a bass pull his lure underneath the water. This was the first time he had invited his college roommate of two years home with him. He hoped he had not made a mistake for both their sakes.

"Yeah, sure I've been fishing before. My uncle used to take me to his, I think its called a farm pond. Why it was called that, I don't know," Jacob added as he finally succeeded in rolling the window down. "Hey, what's this stuff growing in the field. Are those white flowers on top?"

"Jacob, buddy, you are kidding me, right," Matthew asked, trying hard not to laugh. "I know you are not from the south, but surely you know that's cotton. You must have seen cotton fields before?"

"What do you take me for, a dummy, sure I know this is cotton. I just can't see too well. Its not even good daylight yet," the embarrassed young man said.

"That's alright Jacob. Before this day is over, you will learn a lot and experience many special things you've never even imagined," Matthew assured his friend, realizing the day on the river would indeed be a learning experience.

The two rode in silence as Matthew slowly guided the truck around the large holes and ruts that covered the road like a patch-work quilt. Coming up on one that was extremely deep, he stopped and turned the engine off.

"Why are we stopping," Jacob asked as he placed his cap back on his head.

Matthew enjoyed the ride across the field and usually stopped, having a reason to or not. "Just wanted to smell the fresh air and the pungent earth and, "pausing, knowing his friend would think him crazy, Matthew slowly continued, "their presence."

"Smell the earth, feel their presence. Man, are you crazy or something? There's nobody here but us. What are you talking about," Jacob asked, looking around nervously. "This is just a cotton field."

Matthew smiled, a strange look covering his tan face. "Most people would think that, but this is a special place. You see Jacob, this is the land of my people."

"Your people, I didn't know your folks were farmers. Is this your land then," the curious young man asked?

"No, my parents do not own this land. Its much deeper, much older than just today," Matthew continued to smile as he started the engine, the truck and trailer lunging forward. "My ancestors were Creek Indians."

"Oh, cool! Man, you got to tell me all about it. I didn't know you were bringing me on a history trip," Jacob excitedly exclaimed.

"Not a history trip, Jacob, but a trip back to a different time. A time when the native people walked this land and fished this river," Matthew said as the Tallapoosa came into view.

"Oh, man, this is beautiful. Why didn't you tell me it would look like this," Jacob asked as he jumped from the truck? Matthew slowly backed the trailer down the narrow makeshift boat ramp, yelling for Jacob to hold the rope as the boat smoothly slid into the water. After securing the ice chest and the bag of baloney sandwiches his mother had packed for them, Matthew pushed the boat deeper into the water.

"Hey, Jacob, you are coming with me," Matthew yelled as he jumped in, laughing as his friend barely managed to get inside the boat.

Most of the mist had lifted and the morning sounds of the birds filled the air as the two began their trip down river. The Tallapoosa had a story for Matthew to tell and the young man with a far away look in his eyes began. "Family history has it that my fifth grandfather was a brave warrior. His name was Soaring Eagle and he was chief of the Hillabee people who lived on the upper Tallapoosa. He survived the Battle of Horseshoe Bend, spending many months in search of his wife, Little Flower and their children. Against all odds, they were reunited and after several years had passed returned to their Tallapoosa home. There was even a strange story about an owl. "Matthew dipped the paddle into the shinning water of the river and continued to talk. Neither had picked up their rods. This trip was not about fishing now. Matthew could feel, and he hoped his friend would too, the spirit of the people who called the Tallapoosa River Valley home.

Part One
Seasons of Change

Chapter Two
The Horseshoe Revisited

Standing in shocked silence, the motley group of forlorn travelers gazed at the stark remains of the Horseshoe battle site. Five seasons had passed since the tragic events of that day had changed the life of the Hillabee and of all Creek people. The barricade was still in place, the large logs broken where the white soldiers had stormed the structure. Green scrub brush had sprouted and covered the ground and early season wild flowers in shades of yellow and blue dotted the battlefield. Some of them barely covering the now bleached bones of the slain warriors that had not been removed or thrown into the river.

Just past the battlefield, were the remains of the partially burned village, logs from the huti lay in disarray, clay cups and bowls still as the women and children had left them when they had been herded up like the cattle of the white man. Overwhelmed by memories and sorrow, the women, one by one, began the age-old keening of the grandmothers.

Tears filled his own eyes as Soaring Eagle watched his people relive the horrors of that day. He was fortunate, he still had his family, his beautiful, strong wife, Little Flower and his twins, Little Deer and Red Fox. These people had lost so much and to see the battle site again was like a dagger piercing their hearts and souls all over again.

Feeling a touch on his shoulder, the warrior turned to see the mother of his wife, Sunflower Woman. The deep pools of her dark eyes showing the sorrows of not only the present, but of all the grandmothers from the long ago past. She looked at Soaring Eagle and softly asked, "May I be allowed to speak to our people?"

Soaring Eagle nodded, realizing that she would know the right words to say, words that would give them comfort.

Tucking the long strands of her now totally gray hair behind her ear and taking a deep breath, she began, "My family, my friends, you are my people. Listen to what I have to say." One by one the women ceased their keening, their attention on the woman who had been their strength through many seasons of sorrow. "Seeing this place makes my heart bleed. I long for the touch of my husband and the smile of my son, but they are no longer here. They, like the husbands and sons of many of you, have walked the path to the Great Spirit. When we were forced to leave here, we vowed to honor our men. We vowed to come back to our homes here on this river. Our life has changed, and I feel in my heart that more changes will come. Changes that will not be good and changes that will bring us more sorrow." Pausing, a chilly wind began to blow as the sun slid behind the clouds. Before Sunflower Woman could continue, the eerie cry of the owl filled the air.

"No, no, not the owl," one of the women cried out. The cries of the owl had been omens of misfortune and death in the past and the Creek people cringed in fear each time the ominous cry was heard.

The sorrow-filled group began murmuring among themselves as the sound of the owl grew louder and then they watched in relief when the small creature was seen flying over the treetops, his cry fading away.

"Be calm, do not let the sound of the owl cause us to lose hope," Sunflower Woman pleaded. The crowd of mostly women and children and a few old men became silent again, realizing that this woman did indeed have the strength and wisdom of the grandmothers. "Again, I say that we do not know what we will face in future days. We will do as our grandmothers did before us, we will adapt to the change, we will persevere.

We are people of the Hillabee and of all the other villages along this river. We are people of the Wind Clan and the Bear Clan, we are The People, we are Creek and we will survive.

Soaring Eagle waited briefly before speaking, allowing his people time to grasp and understand what Sunflower Woman had said. "My people, please take the words of our wise grandmother. Know that she speaks the truth. We will follow her words and we will do whatever is required. We will continue to live as the strong people we are, being blessed by the Great Spirit. Come, now let us leave this place of sorrow. Let us move forward to the old village of the Hillabee. We have nearly accomplished our goal that we began many seasons ago. We are home."

The group, gathering their meager belongings, followed Soaring Eagle up the overgrown path that led to the Hillabee village site. They were relieved to leave this place of sorrow and anticipated better times in their former town. Here, at least, they would be free and slaves to no one. They would listen to the words of Sunflower Woman and follow the leadership of Soaring Eagle. No matter how difficult, they would rebuild and renew their lives. The women and children as well as the men could not help but smile as the happy song of the blue bird filled the crisp air as they began the final part of their journey.

Chapter Three
Hillabee Home

The weary travelers obviously experienced sadness as they viewed the remnants of their village. Soaring Eagle was relieved when he saw the smile on the face of Sunflower Woman as she began to sing one of the joyful songs of the grandmothers. One by one all the women joined in as tears of happiness instead of sorrow ran down their tired brown faces. They were home. They understood life would not be the same and there would be constant reminders of the joy they had once shared with their husbands and sons and the sadness of their loss. The Hilabee people were ready now to move forward with their life.

In an amazingly short time the Hillabee Village area was cleaned of the debris that covered the ground, fires were built, and the meal was prepared. Each and every one had contributed, the women and children and the old men. Three or four young warriors had joined the group and they along with Soaring Eagle had done most of the heavier work.

Before the fatigued people began their meal of turtle stew and bread made from dried corn, Soaring Eagle stood. The strong, brave man had been the chief of all the Hillabee during the brief period between the massacre of the Hillabee mother town and the time of the Horseshoe. He had fought valiantly and would not have survived had it not been the will of the Great Spirit and the old medicine man, Wolf Fella. He and the old man had become great friends and Soaring Eagle greatly depended on his guidance and assistance. After saving him from certain death, Wolf Fella had not been far from the side of the warrior. He sat now watching him closely as Soaring Eagle began to speak.

"My people, my Hillabee people," Soaring Eagle paused, overcome by emotion, "We are home. This is the day we hoped would come. We have traveled to the great river of Flowered

Rocks and back. We have experienced much sadness and sorrow during the five seasons since we gathered around our Hillabee fire. I do not know what the future will hold for us or for any of the Creek people. The white man is not gone, many more of them will come. More treaties have been signed by some of our leaders, giving the white families more of the land that was once the home of our people. No longer do the proud Red Stick Warriors fight to save our land. They are gone." Soaring Eagle paused, trying to regain his composure. He continued to look out at his people, knowing they depended on his strength and needed for him to have a positive attitude. He could not allow them to sink back into a low place again. "Please forgive me for talking of the sad times. I will now put that time away as we begin our new life at our old home. We are fortunate to have this opportunity. I would like to say thank you for your perseverance and for trusting in me. I know it is the will of the Great Spirit, the Giver of Breath that we are all here together. Now, let us have our food and then rest. We will have much work on the new day. Again, I say, we are home," Soaring Eagle finished as he took the hand of his wife, Little Flower.

    The two walked around the group of fatigued people. Soaring Eagle stopping to talk briefly with each family, offering encouraging words and making sure they were comfortable. His people, as he called them, had varied in numbers over the years. After the Horseshoe, when the Hillabee women had been taken captive to Coweta Town by the White Stick Warriors, his group had been small, but continued to grow as others joined them. Some had stayed with clan members at the small villages they passed along the way, others had been too sick and weak to continue. These were buried by the path. Some of the people who had traveled with him did not have the strength and stamina to return to their homes. These people had remained on the Chattahoochee. Most of the women and children who had been enslaved at Coweta had not been freed to come back to the Tallapoosa.

After checking on all his people, Soaring Eagle and Little Flower joined Sunflower Woman, the twins and the young warrior Horse Stealer who had been waiting by the fire.

"I have our stew and bread ready," Sunflower Woman said as she began dipping the hot stew into the tin plates. "When we rebuild our village, I intend to make clay bowls again. Then all our food will taste like it did in the time before the white people came."

"I agree mother," Little Flower said, passing around the plates to her family. "I too would like to live as we did before they came."

Smiling sadly at his beautiful wife, Soaring Eagle remarked, "Both of you know we can not go back to the time of our grandmothers. We will preserve what we can of our way of life. I do fear we have been caught up in the waves of change the white people have created." Soaring Eagle and his family were silent, each of them reflecting on the words of the strong warrior. With love shining in his eyes, Soaring Eagle looked at his wife and smiled again at his children, who he suddenly realized were not children any longer. "I have been so blessed by the Great Spirit. I have my family. We are together, while so many of our people no longer are with the people they love." Pausing and slightly embarrassed, he continued, "I was fortunate to be reunited with you and travel home again to our Hillabee Town.

Realizing that what the husband of her daughter was experiencing was both physical and emotional fatigue, Sunflower Woman gently said, "We have all been blessed by the Great Spirit to have you to lead and guide us home. Now it is time for us to rest. As you have said, we will have a busy new day."

The young warrior called Horse Stealer had heard the words of Soaring Eagle and Sunflower Woman. He too realized the strength of the warrior and of the woman. He knew without that strength none of the group of people would have been able to make the trip from his former home on the Chattahoochee. He had been banned from Coweta Town after a trumped-up altercation with a white trader. He still swelled with pride when he thought of the time when had stepped between Soaring Eagle and the brave White Stick Warrior, Badger. One or both surely would have been killed. After the Horseshoe, with orders from General Jackson, Badger had taken the Hillabee women and children to Coweta. Along the way, he had fallen deeply in love with the beautiful wife of Soaring Eagle, who had come in search of his family. When the two warriors met, face-to-face, Little Flower had been innocently in the arms of Badger. Horse Stealer had intervened. After hearing the explanation, the jealous husband and rejected warrior both gained respect for each other. Badger arranged for the family of Soaring Eagle and several others to be released from Coweta Town. They then began the seasons-long journey back to the Tallapoosa. Badger had advised Horse Stealer to leave Coweta. As he was well acquainted with the family, the young warrior was happy to accompany them. He had been treated like a son by the two women and Soaring Eagle had encouraged him and showed him the path to becoming a true warrior. He and the twins shared a special bond, having had quite an adventure together. He was only four seasons older than they were, making them fifteen summers.

    Little Deer was always with them, showing both up with her hunting ability and humor. He thought of Red Fox as a brother but was finding it more and more difficult to think of Little Deer as a sister. He looked at her now as she scraped her stew from her plate with the bread of corn. As if knowing the young warrior was watching her and what he was thinking, Little Deer looked up at Horse Stealer and quickly looked away, a slight pink covering her brown face.

    "Soaring Eagle, I agree with our grandmother," Horse Stealer confessed. "The Great Spirit has blessed each of us to be under your guidance. You have made this journey possible. Together we will rebuild your home and your people." Pausing and again looking at the daughter of Soaring Eagle, he said emotionally, "OUR people will once again be happy as we return to the old way. I will be ready to help accomplish this with the new day," the young warrior said as he reached for his blanket and moved a short distance away from the family.

Chapter Four
Wagon Full of Children

Before brother moon was full again, the Hillabee men had reclaimed more of the old village site from the thick woods that had lined the creek. Trees had been cut, using the metal axe of the white man. It had been decided that their new homes would be constructed from logs instead of the less-sturdy huti that had been used in the past. The women and children had helped to clear and plant the barren fields that had laid waste for many seasons. Soon these same fields would be filled with ripened corn and beans and no one would be hungry. The Hillabee people had settled into a busy routine and they were once again content. More people from other villages that had been destroyed during the times of the battle had joined with the Hillabee increasing the size of the town considerably.

Soaring Eagle finding himself resuming the role as chief, also found that the responsibility was greater with a different range of problems. White settlers in wagons with their children hanging onto the side were seen more frequently now that the Alabama Territory had been created. Occasionally these settlers and their wagons crossed over into Indian land with no regard to what the consequences might be. This situation had the potential to be explosive.

Soaring Eagle slowed his black pony to a walk as he saw the white man slide off his own horse and motion for a boy, no more than ten or twelve to follow him. The man slowly raised his musket, taking aim at a large rabbit. Soaring Eagle quickly yelled out, the frightened rabbit scampering into the bushes. Turning to see the Creek warrior, the startled man then pointed his gun at Soaring Eagle. "That rabbit was gonna be supper for me and my family. Now we won't have nutt'n to eat. Why'd you do that, you sneaking injun," the white man asked as his finger tightened on the trigger. "Reckon I'm just gonna haf to shoot you fer that."

"Put your gun down. You are on Creek land. You have no right to be here or to take food from my family," Soaring Eagle calmly said.

"I don't care," the man angrily yelled. "My family's hungry."

Horse Stealer and Red Fox had been behind Soaring Eagle just out of view. Both quickly sprang into action, the older aiming his musket at the white man and Red Fox, always ready with his bow and arrow, pointed his weapon at the boy. "White man," Horse Stealer quietly said, "drop your gun now or you and the boy will die."

Totally unaware of the two, the startled man lowered his gun. "I, I weren't really gonna shoot nobody. Please don't hurt my boy," the man whimpered, "please."

Soaring Eagle, after accessing the situation, noticed the tears in the eyes of the boy and the damp that stained his ragged britches. Feeling sorrow for the man and his pitiful son, he looked briefly back at his companions and smiled, "I knew the two of you had me covered. You can lower your gun and bow now." Looking back at the man and making sure that he too had lowered his gun, he continued, "I am Soaring Eagle, chief of the Hillabee. It is our land that you are on. Did you not realize that? Did you not know that white men are not allowed here? I think it best that you put your gun on the ground and tell your son," looking again at the boy who stood sobbing like a baby, "that we will not harm you."

The white man laid his musket down and looked at his son, ashamed of his behavior. He would never admit that he too could have behaved in the same manner. "I did not know this was Indian land. Me and my woman and five other young'uns is going to Mississippi. We got kin folk over there. We'll just be on our way now, if you don't mind," the man said watching the dark hard eyes of the one called Soaring Eagle.

"Pa," the boy said in a whisper, "Maw said we had to bring back som'in to eat. She said the baby can't last much longer without food."

"Hush boy, we'll make do," the man said. Still not knowing if the Creek man would let them go.

"What name do you go by," Soaring Eagle asked in a cold voice.

"Name is Jones, Willie Jones."

"Jones, I do not believe you did not know this is Creek land and I do believe you would have killed me," Soaring Eagle answered. "I do not want for children, even white children to be hungry. My own children have had to do without food. Where is your family," the chieftain asked?

"Just over the hill there," Jones pointed.

"Horse Stealer go see if there is a wagon and a family over there. Red Fox, go back to our village and ask your mother for some dried corn and bread," Soaring Eagle ordered. "I will stay here and inform this intruder of the danger he and his family are in if they remain inside Creek land." Hoping to frighten him more than he already was, the Hillabee chieftain knew that even though the white man was trespassing, there would most likely be more problems for his people if this white family were harmed.

Horse Stealer quickly returned, confirming that there was indeed a wagon full of screaming white children and a tired-looking woman that seemed on the verge of hysteria. Red Fox had secured food for the hungry white family and Soaring Eagle had once more informed Jones that he should leave Creek land as soon as possible.

"What is the best route to go," Jones questioned, realizing that the next injun he met up with might not be as helpful as this one.

"Continue moving in the direction of the setting sun," Soaring Eagle answered, relieved that the man and his bunch of hollering children would be leaving. "You will come to a river, the Coosa. It is too wide and deep to ford. There are ferries that will get you across. When you reach the other side, you will be in Alabama Territory and you will have safe travel

Just A Cotton Field

then. Your days will be many before you reach the place called Mississippi."

"Much obliged, uh, for the food and the directions," the man called Jones stammered, "and for not killing me and my family."

"I wish for you to be safe," the valiant warrior honestly answered. "I hope you do not meet up with any other Creek along the way. If you do, do not point your musket at them," Soaring Eagle said pointedly, "understand? I think now you should be on your way. Red Fox, give me the other pouch of corn you have." The young warrior gave his father the pouch he had been holding as he eyed the white boy and his siblings. "Take this dried corn. Mix it with water and you will at least have food," Soaring Eagle said. "Now go."

"Thank you again," Jones said admiringly. "This injun was different, he was not a savage like most of 'em."

Chapter Five
Eyes for No Other

Soaring Eagle and the two young warriors watched as the motley family piled back into the rickety old wagon. Two old cane back chairs and various cooking utensils hung loosely on the side. Jones threw up his hand in farewell as he cracked his whip across the back of two skinny mules that struggled to move with the heavy load, the wide-eyed children still cowering with fright.

Horse Stealer shook his head in disbelief as he watched the travelers move slowly out of sight. "And we let people like that take our land away," he added.

Soaring Eagle laughed, "If they all were like Jones and his family, all of the land of the grandfathers would still belong to us. Unfortunately, many of the white eyes are much more intelligent."

"Father, do you think he would have shot you if Horse Stealer and me had not been there," Red Fox asked?

"Did you see the condition of his old musket," Soaring Eagle asked, laughing again. "I do not think it would fire and if it did, the aim of Jones would not have been true." Becoming serious Soaring Eagle continued, "I do not think the Jones family will make it to the place called Mississippi. They will either starve or some of our not-so-kind brothers will have their way with them. Their bones will be scattered along the path even before they reach the Coosa." This sad prediction from Soaring Eagle would indeed become an actuality. "Come, your mother and grandmother will be waiting for our return and they will have more than dried corn for us to eat."

After the meal of roasted deer and sofkee laced with honey had been eaten, Red Fox announced that he and Horse Stealer planned to go up White Oak Creek to get the white clay that Sun Flower Woman had requested. Tired of helping her mother and grandmother with routine work, Little Deer excitedly exclaimed that she was going with her brother and Horse Stealer.

Soaring Eagle and his wife exchanged glances. "I think it best for you to stay here and help your mother and grandmother, Little Deer," her father said, seeing the instant disappointment in the eyes of his defiant daughter.

"Father, I have worked very hard today and I am tired of always doing the work of the women," Little Deer blurted out.

"My daughter, you will be a woman soon and you should learn these things," Little Flower said. Also seeing the disappointment in the eyes of Horse Stealer.

Watching the scene develop before her, Sun Flower Woman smiled and said, "I think the child needs a rest from this woman's work. I think that I too will go to my huti," pausing the older woman asked, "What do you call this place where we live, this place like the ones of the white-skinned people?"

"A log cabin, grandmother," Red Fox said, turning to look at his parents, "I would like for Little Deer to come with us," smiling at his friend and his sister. "She can help us find the best clay for the bowls and cups. The three of us enjoy spending time together."

Giving into the wishes of the young people, Soaring Eagle looked up at the position of the sun and then at the trees that lined the creek bank. "I need for you to be back, right here when brother sun falls behind those trees. Understand me? It is not safe to be that far from the village when the darkness of night begins to come. There is the possibility of more white people like Jones. No, people smarter than he was, could be lurking around," Soaring Eagle smiled at Little Flower and reached for her hand. "I think I would like a rest from work this day too. Come, my beautiful wife. Let us go for a walk as well," looking at the young warrior and his children, Soaring Eagle continued, "Remember, be back here before the sun sets." Soaring Eagle and Little Flower, hand in hand went one direction while Horse Stealer and the twins went the other, their laughter reverberating throughout the woods.

"Little Flower, "Soaring Eagle said sadly, "You know that our son will soon be a warrior and our daughter will become a beautiful young maiden, just like her mother." Pausing he lifted the face of his wife and tenderly kissed her.

"Yes, I realize these things and, also I know that it is nearing the time for Horse Stealer to take a wife and that he has eyes for no other but Little Deer," Little Flower said, her eyes shining with unshed tears.

"She is too young! She is not yet ready to be a wife to Horse Stealer or any other warrior," the emotional father said.

"Before the yellow tassels appear on the new corn, our children will have seen fifteen summers. Many young maidens take husbands at that age and our son should already have his warrior name. You and I chose to wait longer before we had our marriage celebration," pausing Little Flower smiled sweetly at her husband, "But, you do remember the love we shared even at that age, do you not?"

Shaking his head in affirmative, Soaring Eagle did indeed remember the deep love he and Little Flower had shared for so many years. "I do. Times were so uncertain then. War with the white man was eminent. We did not know what the future would hold. We still do not know that do we," he asked with a whimsical smile, "we know from the past that the white man speaks with a forked tongue. They say this," pausing to spread his arms, "is our land and the whites cannot harm us or take it away now. I fear this is not true. More and more white men and their families will come inside the nation. They kill the few deer that remains and take the food that belongs to us. The time will soon be when they will take from us this land. Our own people will sign the papers of the white man that will give our land to them." Looking at his wife, seeing the same look of fear that he had seen on her face many seasons past, he kissed her again," I am sorry, my Little Flower. I did not intend to say words that would frighten you. Come, let us continue our walk and speak of happy times when we were young and our love was new.

Just A Cotton Field

Chapter Six
Fox Slayer

Using the directions from his grandmother, Red Fox led the way as he, Little Deer and Horse Stealer walked far up White Oak Creek. The trees became dense and thick, the sunlight weakly filtering to the forest floor. "Look, there is the place grandmother talked about. See how the water runs down from the hillside making clay that is white as frost in the time of the cold moon," Red Fox excitedly exclaimed, urging his sister and friend to catch up with him. "Why are the two of you so far behind? We have much work to do to get the clay for our grandmother."

Horse Stealer laughed as he and Little Deer joined Red Fox. "Your sister spotted a small cedar sprout and decided she would cross the creek herself to dig it from the ground. I had to help her back across."

"No, you decided that yourself," Little Deer answered, her eyes twinkling with amusement. "I can cross any creek by myself."

"So, why is your skirt wet?" Horse Stealer asked. "Come. Can I help get the clay, or do you want to do that by yourself too?"

Shaking her head, Little Deer ordered, "You dig the clay from the ground and I will place it in my pouch."

"You two dig here and I will walk just a little farther up the creek. There could be more good clay," Red Fox called out as he began walking.

The young warrior had been gone for only a short while when he heard a strange yep coming from the direction that he had just come. Turning, he heard the sound again. Pulling his bow from his shoulder Red Fox began to run, fearing for his sister and friend.

Little Deer and Horse Stealer where both on their knees

occupied with the task of gathering the clay. The gurgling of the stream drowning out the sound of the large gray fox as it staggered toward them, white foam dripping from its mouth. "Horse Stealer, Little Deer," Red Fox yelled as he quickly notched and released the arrow from his bow. The rabid animal leaped into the air and fell at the feet of Horse Stealer, the arrow protruding from its side.

All three stood in fearful silence. The quick action of Red Fox had saved his sister and friend from certain death had the creature attacked them. Horse Stealer could feel the cold sweat form on his forehead and the tremble of Little Deer at his side. He turned and placed his arms around the stunned girl. "Come, little one. We must leave this place. I feel the presence of evil here now," Horse Stealer said softly, feeling he needed to protect both Little Deer and her brother. "Red Fox, now you are my brother. You have saved both of us. Let us return to our villager, shadows of the night are beginning to fall."

The young people hastily begin their return trip to Hillabee Town. The laughter they had shared earlier had been replaced with a somber quiet. All of them understood how close they had come to tragedy. The bite from any rabid animal was usually fatal with the victim suffering a slow agonizing death. They had not walked far when a sudden chilling wind began to blow. The sun dipped behind the treetops and the mournful cry of the owl filled the silence. The twins stopped and looked at each other. This was the cry of the owl their father, mother and grandmother had talked about. Horse Stealer too knew of the dark omens of the owl.

"The owl cannot hurt us," Horse Stealer quietly whispered. "Just keep walking. We do not need to delay any longer. We still have much farther to go and the sun will be below the horizon before we return home."

Little Deer looked at Horse Stealer, her eyes filling with tears. "I am afraid. I have never felt this fear before. Please make it go away, Horse Stealer."

The young warrior felt his heart flutter as he looked at

Little Deer. Instantly remembering the brave little girl that he had taken captive many seasons ago. "Do not be afraid little one," the young warrior said, taking her hand, noticing that she still clasped the pouch of clay in the other. "The danger is over now."

The sun had dropped from the sky and twilight had settled in and the three-young people had still not returned home. Little Flower and Sun Flower Woman had the evening meal prepared and the village people were beginning to settle down for the time of darkness. Little Flower looked at her husband, a look of worry covering her still youthful face. "My husband, they should be home. Something must have happened. Do you think you should go look for them?"

Always relying on her wisdom of many seasons, Sun Flower woman calmly remarked to her daughter, "It is possible that they went far up the creek and it is taking longer to return than they expected, and," smiling, "We know how the three of them enjoy being together."

"That is possible," Soaring Eagle said as he picked up his musket. "They were instructed to be back here before the sun dropped behind the trees. I will go in search of them."

"Here they come," Little Flower joyfully exclaimed, her happiness quickly turning to concern when she saw the faces of the three-young people. "My children, what is wrong?"

Little Deer ran to her mother, falling into her arms. "A crazy fox, oh mother," she sobbed. "And, and, we heard the owl."

"Come, children. Sit down and tell what has happened. Are you hurt," Sun Flower Woman asked anxiously?"

The twins looked at Horse Stealer indicating that he should relay the events of what had happened. "We found the clay our grandmother told us about. Little Deer and me were digging the clay and Red Fox had walked farther up the creek," Horse Stealer paused, the fear briefly returning." He heard the crazy fox yep and then hurried back, shooting it with his trusty bow and arrow, just as the animal leaped to attack," the young warrior finished, looking at Red Fox with gratitude.

After a brief silence, Sun Flower Woman quietly asked, "The owl, you heard the owl?"

"Yes, as we were walking back. The owl seemed to follow us. I do not know what this means. I have heard the old ones talk of the owl. I do not think this is a good sign," Horse Stealer replied with a tremor in his strong voice.

Soaring Eagle looked at his son and daughter with love and relief shinning in his eyes. "No, it is never good to hear the owl. We do not know what the future will bring. For now, I am thankful that my son is an excellent marksman with his bow."

"So am I," Horse Stealer said, smiling at Red Fox.

"I think he is so good because of all the practice he had trying to be better than me," Little Deer chimed in, ending a serious mood.

Laughing at his spirited daughter, Soaring Eagle added, "You may be right, but it will not be you who will receive a warrior name when we have the Green Corn Ceremony in the next moon. Your brother will then be called, Fox Slayer.

Chapter Seven
Secrets to Share

Of the seventy-six people who now lived at Hillabee Town, only thirty-two were warriors. Half of those were either old and tired, and still suffered from battle injuries or had not received their warrior name. Many of the women were old enough to be considered grandmothers and most of the women of child-bearing age had lost their husbands either at the Horseshoe or one of the other battles.

The mixed group of old and young, healthy and weak, worked well together, providing ample food and comfortable cabins, each having their own job to do. The cry of the owl had not been heard again and no more crazy fox had ventured near the village.

Soaring Eagle along with Horse Stealer and Red Fox were going down Hillabee Creek to the river in hopes of catching some large yellow catfish for the Green Corn feast. Little Deer had pouted when she was told that she could not go along. "Little Deer," her father admonished, "You cannot always be with your brother and Horse Stealer. You should stay here and help your mother and grandmother. I have noticed your mother seems to tire more easily."

"Yes, my father," Little Deer replied, "I will help." Thinking that his strong-willed daughter was showing more maturity, Soaring Eagle was disappointed when she frowned and added, "I will stay and do the work of a woman, but I know I could catch more fish."

Laughing, Horse Stealer playfully pinched her cheek. "Little Deer, I am sure you can catch more fish, but you need to learn all the skills of being a woman." Becoming serious, he added, "You will soon need those skills."

Soaring Eagle had watched the moment between the two-young people and realized that Horse Stealer had fallen in love with his daughter, just as her mother had said. "Come, let us go," Soaring Eagle said, "We will return before darkness falls and Little Deer you may help prepare the fish for all of us to eat." He saw Horse Stealer turn and smile at Little Deer. Soaring Eagle smiled too as he remembered the love that began between he and her mother long ago.

Little Flower, Sun Flower Woman and a begrudging Little Deer along with Spotted Fawn and her daughter were going to help the other women clean the village square ground. The Green Corn Ceremony would begin in two suns and there was much work to do. This would be the first big ceremony to be held since before the Horse Shoe and the village people were all excited. Word had been sent up and down the Tallapoosa to invite all the small camps of Creek people who had slowly returned home.

Even Little Deer was enjoying herself as the women gossiped and laughed while they swept and cleaned the square ground. To the older women, this brought back good memories of the past when the ritual was celebrated every year. The young maidens, most who did not remember the significance, looked forward to the dancing and the making of new friends.

Sun Flower Woman noticed as Little Flower stopped and wiped the perspiration from her flushed face. "My daughter, do you not feel well this day," the concerned mother asked, fearing her daughter was coming down with some illness.

"Mother, I am just tired," Little Flower paused and smiled, "Very tired. I think I should rest."

Sun Flower Woman looked closely again at the younger woman. Smiling herself she quietly stated, "My daughter, I believe you have a secret to share. I have not seen you visit the huti for the women in the last two months.

"My mother, you do observe much," Little Flower said, smiling broadly. "Yes, I am with child."

Sun Flower Woman, Little Deer and Spotted Fawn all excitedly hugged Little Flower. "I knew that I would have a new sister," Little Deer proclaimed.

"And, just how did you know that, my daughter," Little

Flower asked, wiping tears from her eyes. "And, how do you know that you will not have a brother?"

"I just do. Wait and see," Little Deer laughed. "Oh, my mother, I am so happy."

"I did not think that I could be with child after seeing so many seasons. I pray to the Great Spirit, the Giver of Breath, that I can carry and give birth to a healthy child," Little Deer tearfully replied.

"I too am happy for you and I hope the Great Spirit will also bless me with a child," Spotted Fawn happily said. "I have good words to share now."

The little group of women eagerly turned to the woman who was a part of their family. She and Little Flower had been best friends as children and both had celebrated their marriage on the same day, with Spotted Fawn becoming the wife of Brave Hawk, the brother of Little Flower. "After the Green Corn Ceremony, I will become the wife of Fast Runner," Spotted Fawn informed. "My love for Brave Hawk will live for as long as I see the light of each new day, but he is gone," She continued, as a fleeting look of pain covered her face as she remembered the day of the Horse Shoe.

"My son would want you to again find happiness," Sun Flower Woman whispered, hugging the woman she considered her daughter. "My family, let us return home now."

Chapter Eight
Green Corn Once Again

They came in small groups of three or four and then some larger groups of ten and twenty, all making their way to Hillabee Town. Each one bringing roasted meat, fresh new corn and other food to contribute to the Green Corn Ceremony feast. Fasting had been done, the town had been cleaned and refreshed and everything was new again. Several seasons had past since there had been celebrations of any kind. There was nothing to celebrate. The wisdom and strong spirit of the Red Stick Women had prevailed. They had proclaimed that now was the time for the Creek people to come together again. The past hardships would never be forgotten, but the women realized if the Creek people were to survive they had to move forward.

The excitement grew as the Hillabee Town continued to fill with other Creek people. Some were total strangers while many were old friends or family members that had not been seen since before the time of the battle. The noticeably small number of young children screamed in delight as they ran and played. The young maidens, coyly flirted with the young warriors as they watched them show off their various skills. Their numbers were also small. The older women and grandmothers laughed as they gossiped and then became strangely quiet and sober when a special poignant memory of a love one who was no longer with them was remembered. Talk between the warriors and old men centered around the battles, of what had happened and what they could have done to have had a different outcome.

Soaring Eagle, as chief of the Hillabee and host of the festival watched as the sun slowly climbed to its mid-point in the sky. He knew, probably to the dismay of many, that it was time for the men to speak. At the signal of the drumbeat, he stood, and the crowd became silent.

"My friends, welcome to Hillabee Town," the warrior chief said. "I am pleased to see all of you and I hope you enjoy your stay. This is the first Poskeeta celebrated in many seasons and I am sure there is much that could be said," smiling as he heard the groans coming from the crowd, he continued, "I am not going to say many words. I would like for us to celebrate on this day and begin our time of renewal." Pausing again for the yells of approval which quickly returned to groans again as he asked if anyone wished to speak.

A wrinkled old man stood, leaning heavily on a carved wooden cane, "I would, my son," he said, looking out at the crowd who had again become silent. "I am Wolf Fella. I have been a knower for the Hillabee people since the time of the grandfathers," the old man said, indicating that he had been a medicine man for many seasons. "My words will be short. No need for me to talk of what we have experienced. You know that. I speak of future. Our times of trouble are not over. Dark days will again return. Remember this. The Creek people will survive," the old medicine man firmly proclaimed as he hobbled back to his place in the crowd.

Smiling at his trusted friend, Soaring Eagle asked if anyone had more words to say. The response to his question was silence. "Then let us celebrate."

The festivities last long after the moon had risen high into the night sky. The fresh corn and roasted meat had been consumed in volumes. The old men and warriors had retired to council, drinking their fill of the black drink, accee, while smoke from their pipes encircled their heads. Talk was of the continuing encroachment of the white families who craved the land that was the home of the Creek people.

The beat of the drum signaled the time of the dance, the mature women and grandmothers first taking their turn slowly around the fire. The remaining young maidens were then beckoned to join them, the drum beat intensifying. Just as her mother had done, many seasons before, Little Deer gracefully spun around, her small body moving in perfect unison with the drum beat. Horse Stealer watched as she rounded the circle, their eyes locking, and in that moment, both knew their lives would be forever entwined.

The final dance belonged to the warriors. Red Fox had received his warrior name and was now known as Fox Slayer. He too joined in the dance. As in the past, the movement mimicked that of battle, their knives flashing in the firelight, their war cries sounding in the night. The warriors danced round and round, falling to the ground at the final beat of the drum.

The warriors rose, officially ending the time of the Green Corn Ceremony. Soaring Eagle, panting for breath looked out at the jubilant crowd, "My people, we are one again. The Poskeeta has brought us renewal."

Chapter Nine
Time of the Cold Moon
(February 1820)

Deep pain woke Little Flower. She smiled as then another pain coursed through her lower back. "It is time," She said softly to herself. She awkwardly rolled from the couch she shared with Soaring Eagle, trying not to wake him. She would go to the cabin of her mother. Together they would go to the huti of the women, the place where Hillabee women gave birth. Little Flower pulled her blanket closer as she went out into the cold, the light of the brother moon shinning brightly in the night sky. After taking only a few short steps, the stab of pain filled her body. As she sank to the ground, Little Flower heard the haunting sound of the owl. "Not the owl, oh please not the owl," she whispered.

The old medicine man, taking his nightly walk to make sure all was well in the village, heard the owl and the whimpers of a woman. Knowing he was near the cabin of Soaring Eagle, Wolf Fella knew that it was Little Flower who needed help. He quickly ran to her side. "Little Flower, Little Flower."

"Wolf Fella, please help me," the weak woman faintly said. "It is my time, I fear for my child and myself. Please help," Little Flower said, closing her eyes as another hard pain consumed her body, the cry of the owl becoming louder.

Wolf Fella quickly yelled out for Soaring Eagle. "Come, you need hurry. Go for Sun Flower Woman." Her swollen belly making it more difficult, the old man slowly picked up the woman he loved as a daughter. He knew that her condition was serious, and he did not know if he could save the child or the mother.

Seeing his wife in the arms of Wolf Fella, Soaring Eagle's heart sank. "Little Flower, oh my Flower," the warrior chieftain exclaimed.

"No time talk. Go for Sun Flower Woman. Need fire at huti of women," Wolf Fella demanded as he struggled to carry Little Flower who lay listless in his arms.

Sweat broke out on the face of Soaring Eagle as he ran to the small cabin of the mother of his wife. "Oh, Great Spirit, please let my Little Flower live," the frightened husband said out loud as he banged on the side of Sun Flower Woman's cabin. "Sun Flower Woman, my mother, come quick," he yelled.

Sun Flower Woman came out of her cabin, pulling on her moccasins as she ran. She knew without being told that this was about her daughter and she realized that she was in danger. "Where is she?" the anxious mother asked.

"Wolf Fella took her to he huti for the women," Soaring Eagle replied. "He said he needs fire. Oh, Sun Flower Woman. I am so afraid. I cannot lose my Flower."

"Be calm, Soaring Eagle. We do not yet know the situation. Giving birth to a child can at times be difficult. She will need your strength if there is a problem. Wolf Fella and me will know what to do. Let us hurry," Sun Flower Woman wisely said, trying to calm the warrior and herself as well.

Wolf Fella had placed Little Flower on a couch and covered her with several blankets. He quickly took his medicine from the beaded pouch he wore around his neck. Pulling his medicine stick from his belt, he immediately began the age-old procedure. The old medicine man chanted the words of the grandfathers through his stick. He then gently blew into the water-filled bowl that contained his medicine. The words and medicine would join to make his medicine strong.

Soaring Eagle and Sun Flower Woman followed by Little Deer had reached the huti. Sun Flower Woman ordered Soaring Eagle to start the fire just outside the huti and for Little Deer to bring water from the nearby spring. She then allowed herself to go to her daughter. "Little Flower, my child, look at me," the wise woman ordered as she picked up her hand. Little Flower opened her eyes and forced a tiny smile as another pain crashed down upon her.

"Oh, oh," she cried out. "My mother, I am not sure I can do this much longer. Will my baby come soon?" Little Flower whispered, clinching her mother's hand.

Sun Flower woman pressed her daughter's stomach and frowned. "The baby is not yet in the right position. It will take more time."

Little Flower closed her eyes as tears of both pain and fear ran down her drawn face, "I need to see my Eagle. I need to see Soaring Eagle."

Nodding her head in approval, Sun Flower Woman raised the skin flap and beckoned for the husband of her daughter to come.

Seeing the worried look on Sun Flower Woman's face, Soaring Eagle quickly rushed to his wife's side. "My Flower," he said as he gently wiped the sweat and tears from her face. "Be strong, please be strong. This will be over soon." Soaring Eagle heard the words of the old medicine man and saw him blow into the medicine bowl. He had never felt such fear.

"My son, I think you should go now. Your wife not need to see your fear," Wolf Fella said, turning to look at Little Flower who had again cried out in pain.

"Wolf Fella, will my wife see the light of the new sun," the anxious warrior asked softly, not wanting her to hear.

"Time will tell. I will do as I did for you in your time of pain and injury. I will do my best. Go," the old medicine man said as he began chanting again.

Fox Slayer and Horse Stealer and many other village people who lived near Soaring Eagle and Little Flower had gathered around the fire. Little Deer having been told to stay outside with the others, took her place beside her father. The wind blew cold and the stars twinkled in the night sky. The continued chanting of the old medicine man, the painful moaning of Little Flower and the chilling cry of the owl filled the air. Some of the women began keening, fearing what the sound meant for their beloved Little Flower.

"My father," Little Deer began, only to be silenced by Horse

Stealer as he took her hand into his.

"My little one, you are cold. Come let me warm you," the young warrior said, wrapping his blanket around the shivering maiden. "Do not cry."

The moon slid lower in the sky and still Soaring Eagle and his family waited. The chants and the owl's cry had continued and then suddenly…silence. Soaring Eagle looked into the sky, seeing the dim light of a morning star. "Great Spirit, Giver of Breath," the fearful man whispered, "Please spare the life of Little Flower and that of our child."

Several minutes passed and still no sound came from inside the huti. Tears formed in the eyes of the women and one of the old grandmothers began an ancient chant of sorrow. A shadow passed overhead amidst a flutter of wings as the owl flew and the mournful call from a distant coyote was heard. Not knowing the fate of his wife, Soaring Eagle rushed toward the huti, stopping short when he heard a deep moan from the woman he loved, and then…the loud cry of a baby.

Tears of joy ran down his face as he stood just outside, knowing that he would be told to wait, certain things had to be done before he would be allowed to see his wife and new child. He impatiently waited to be called in. Hearing nothing but the loud wale of the baby, Soaring Eagle was instantly gripped with new fear. What if the baby lived and his Little Flower had not? What if…Chants from the old medicine man again broke the intense silence. Waiting no longer, the frantic husband rushed inside the huti.

The look of fear on Sun Flower Woman's face relayed the seriousness of the situation. Motioning for him to come, Soaring Eagle quickly went to his wife's side. "Little Flower, oh my Flower," he softly said as he took her clammy hand into his. Filling his touch and hearing his voice, she slowly opened her eyes, smiling weakly at her husband. She did not attempt to speak. Looking up at Wolf Fella, Soaring Eagle silently asked if his wife would live. The old medicine man again chanted into his medicine stick and blew into the water bowl.

Sun Flower Woman touched him on his shoulder, indicating that she wished to speak with him. Slowly releasing Little Flower's hand and gently stroking her strained but beautiful face, Soaring Eagle turned to the mother of his wife. "Soaring Eagle, my son, the condition of my daughter is grave. Wolf Fella tells me if we can cool her body, she will live, if not," the strong woman's voice broke and she quickly wiped the tears from her face that now looked old and tired. "We need for you to tell Little Deer and Fox Slayer to go down by the creek and bring back much bear grass. This will remove the heat," pausing again she smiled. "Come, look, see your new daughter. She is strong and healthy. She will need nourishment soon. Go and tell her sister and brother to hurry with the bear grass. Ask the Great Spirit to spare the mother of this new child, so that she too can live."

Realizing that his wife had again drifted back into a restless sleep, he gently kissed her cheek. He brushed the tears from his own eyes and looked inquiringly at the old medicine man.

"My son," Wolf Fella said softly, "She weak, very weak. Heat must leave her body," he smiled, hoping to relieve the fear of the man he thought of as his son. "I feel in my heart she will live to see," he pointed at the baby, "the children of new child. Come and see her and then go. Do not come back until I call for you. I must make strong medicine."

Feeling weak himself, Soaring Eagle turned and faced Sun Flower Woman and the loudly crying child. As he looked at his daughter, the baby instantly stopped crying, her black eyes seeming to focus on her father. Soaring Eagle was surprised and startled to see the strength of not only Little Flower in the eyes of the baby, but also the strength of the grandmothers. He knew then that both this child and her mother would live.

Just A Cotton Field

Chapter Ten
1825 – Time of New Leaves

"My father, why can I not go with you," the little girl asked, her lower lip quivering as she pulled on her father's leg. "Please let me go."

"You can not always go with me," Soaring Eagle answered, swinging the child high in the air. "You know that I have important things to do."

"Father, please. I will be good," she begged, her huge brown eyes twinkling with tears as she wrapped her arms around his neck.

"Morning Star, not this time," Soaring Eagle said tenderly as he put her down. "I need for you to help your mother and sister today."

More than four seasons had passed since the night of long, hard labor for Little Flower. Despite the ominous warning of the owl, Little Flower, slow to regain her strength had completely recovered and the baby grew to be a healthy and strong little girl.

Soaring Eagle, seeing the light of a morning star as he had asked the Great Spirit to allow his wife and child to live, had insisted her name would be Morning Star. The child soon became a delight to not only her father, but to all the Hillabee people. She was quick to learn and even though very strong-willed, was obedient and never created any problem. The people talked of the look of strength in her eyes. Many saying that the child was special and would be an example of strength for the Creek people during troubling times.

Little Flower, seeing the child's disappointment in not being allowed to go with her father, quickly came to her husband's rescue. "Come, my child. Today we will go up the Creek and dig some nice orange clay to make pretty new bowls." Many of the Hillabee families, including Little Flower, had some of the blue and white dishes of the white women, but she insisted on still making the bowls and pots in the traditional way of the Creek people. "And I will allow you to use one of my favorite stamps to press the decorations on the bowls. Will that not be a good time for us," Little Flower asked, taking the little girl's hand. Pausing to kiss her husband on his cheek, she continued, "Your father needs to talk with many of the warriors today."

"Yes, I do," the chieftain answered his wife. "We will make our plans to go down river to Tuckabachee Town. Many will come from far away for council." He patted the dark head of his daughter. "Morning Star, do as your mother ask this day."

"Yes, my father," the little child said, forgetting her disappointment. "Mother, can Little Deer and grandmother Sun Flower go with us?"

"Yes, together we can dig much clay," the wise mother said as she smiled at Soaring Eagle, love shinning in her eyes. "Come, let us first go to the house of grandmother and then to get Little Deer."

Sun Flower Woman was delighted to join her daughter and granddaughter in their adventure. Having seen the season of new leaves well over sixty times, she had experienced much change in the lives of her people. To make bowls of clay as the grandmothers of the past had done, brought her happiness, but also made her sad. In the wisdom she had gained during her lifetime, Sun Flower Woman knew the old ways were rapidly disappearing and would never more return.

Morning Star excitedly ran ahead to the house of Little Deer and Horse Stealer. The couple had been married in the traditional Creek way during the time of Poskeeta after the birth of her little sister. As with her parents, Little Deer and Horse Stealer's love began when they were young. They both laughed of the time when the inexperienced Horse Stealer had taken Little Deer and her brother, Red Fox captive, then sobered when they talked of the adventures and fear they had experienced. In their quiet moments, Horse Stealer would hold his wife close and tell her how he had been enamored by the brave, spirited little girl.

"Little Deer, Little Deer," Morning Star called out. "Come with us. We are going to walk by the Creek. Our mother said we can dig for some clay and make pots."

Little Deer quickly came out of her house, wiping her hands on a newly acquired red apron, more evidence of the influence of the white people and how the Creek women were adapting to this new way. "My Star, my Little Star," the older sister answered as she picked up the child and hugged her. The two shared an uncommon, close bond for siblings so far apart in age. Little Deer often reminded her family of how she had known her mother would give birth and that the child would be a girl. In the first season of cold after she and Horse Stealer had married, a baby had come to soon and could not survive. Little Deer knew the child she now carried would be a boy as she placed her hand on her stomach and smiled, feeling the flutter of life within her. "Oh, Star, come quick and feel. The baby is kicking. I know he will become a strong, brave warrior just like his father," the young woman said, laughing at the look of delight on her baby sisters face. "Come mother and grandmother. I want you to feel the new life of our people."

The baby continued to kick long enough for the women to feel the movement and both had tears of joy in their eyes. This child would indeed be a symbol of life for the Creek people. "What is this about going to dig for clay?" Little Deer asked.

"I think we need to make new bowls and pots. I would like clay from up White Oak Creek. Do you feel like going with us today," Little Flower asked, looking at her daughter closely?

"Yes, Horse Stealer has gone with father and Fox Slayer to meet with the other headmen. He said they have much to discuss about a trip to Tuckabatchee. I was just getting ready to skin a rabbit for stew. I can do that later. This trip will be good," Little Deer happily said as she untied the apron. "My grandmother, do you like my new apron? Horse Stealer traded the skin of two foxes for it."

"No, I do not like the cloth. You are not a white woman,"

Sun Flower Woman said sharply. Seeing the hurt look on the face of her granddaughter, the older woman quickly continued, "I am sorry Little Deer. Your apron, as it is called, is very nice. I am deeply saddened by the rapid change that has taken place in the past few seasons and it disturbs me that my own family has accepted the change so easily. Come, let us go up the White Oak Creek. It will be nice to make new pots. That will remind me of the days of my youth."

"I am hungry," Morning Star said in a little soft voice. "Can we have some food before we go?"

Laughing at the child, Little Flower hugged her daughter. "I think we will take some fried bread with us and sit by the creek to eat. Will that not be better?"

"Yes, my mother. Let us go now," the little girl said, skipping ahead up the well-worn path that led to White Oak Creek.

Chapter Eleven
Home, Sweet Home

The women and little girl, laughing and talking as they walked, slowly made their way up the path to the place of orange clay. They sat on a moss-covered log eating their fried bread as the water gurgled past them in its continuous route to the Tallapoosa.

"My grandmother," Little Deer said as she finished her bread. "What do you think the seasons ahead will be like for us? I have listened to your warnings. I have experienced for myself the sorrow of our people and the fear of not knowing from one sun to the next what would be our fate. I worry for my child." Smiling again as she rubbed her stomach, knowing that she soon would be able to hold her baby.

"My child, I cannot give you the answer," Sun Flower Woman sadly answered. "As you said, we have all endured much. I fear there will be more troubling times and much sadness for all of the Creek people." Smiling at Morning Star who had grown tired of sitting on the log, she continued, "I do feel in my heart that the spirit of the grandmothers are with us and that we," she smiled, again pointing to Morning Star who was now happily playing in the shallow water, "and to the child within you, will persevere and endure. Come, let us dig in the bank for the orange clay that we came for."

Having collected enough of the brightly colored clay to make several small bowls, the women and child prepared to return to Hillabee Town. Suddenly hearing singing from farther up the path, Sun Flower Woman placed her finger over her lips and pulled Morning Star to her, keeping the child silent.

"Home, Sweet Home," a deep voice of a man sang as the pleasant voice of a woman joined in. "Over mountains and valleys no more to roam. Be it ever so humble, there's no place like home."

"My mother," Little Flower whispered, "Who?"

"Shh," Sun Flower Woman said, pulling her family down behind a large green bush. They watched, as only a short distance away, on the larger path that led from Oakfuskee to the northern areas of Creek land, a family bounced up and down in a wagon pulled by a single skinny cow.

"Home, Sweet Home," they began again, unaware that they were being watched. The family slowly moved out of sight as they continued farther up the path. "Home, Sweet Home," echoing through the trees.

"My mother," Little Flower began again. "Who are these people? Why were they singing that song? This is our home. It does not belong to them."

Sun Flower Woman frowned as she took Morning Star's hand. "Come, I need to tell Soaring Eagle and the other headmen about these people. There have been reports about an increasing number of white families coming on our land. Up until now they have been just passing through on their way to one of the white towns," She answered. "And no, this is not their home," yet, Sun Flower Woman thought to herself.

After leaving her family in their homes, Sun Flower Woman went straight to the square ground. The chief and headmen were in serious discussion about their upcoming trip down river to Tuckabatchee. It was no surprise to any of them when they saw the woman enter the square ground. Sun Flower Woman was well respected for her wisdom and was considered a Beloved Woman. Her words would be welcomed.

"Sun Flower Woman, my mother," Soaring Eagle said warmly. "It is good to have you join us in council this day. Do you have words you wish to share with us?"

"Yes, my son," the wise older woman said, her voice strong and clear, her eyes warming as she looked directly at the husband of her daughter. "I, my daughter and her children have just returned from a trip up White Oak Creek," she paused, seeing the question in the chieftain's eyes. Smiling she continued, "We went there to dig the orange clay. My young granddaughter should learn how the old ones made their pots."

Smiling as he thought of Morning Star, Soaring Eagle softly said, "This is good. My child should know the old ways."

Smiling herself at the thought of the child splashing in the water with orange clay running down her arms, the Beloved Woman began to speak. "As we were leaving we saw a small white family just up the path. They did not see us," frowning, she finished. "They were singing a song."

"Singing," one of the men asked? "Singing what?"

"A song I had never heard before. I did not like the song," Sun Flower Woman replied.

The headmen waited patiently as Sun Flower Woman composed herself, wiping the tears from her beautiful, sad eyes, "Home, Sweet Home. There's no place like home."

Soaring Eagle and the other headmen sat in silence, the words of their Beloved Woman heavy on their hearts. "In two suns we will join Chief Menawa at Oakfuskee," Soaring Eagle said, with anger in his voice. "Together we will go down river to Tuckabatchee Town."

Chapter Twelve
Down the Tallapoosa

Before the sun rose the following day, Soaring Eagle, Fox Slayer, Horse Stealer and twenty other able-bodied strong warriors began their trek down the Tallapoosa to Oakfuskee. The painful bones of Wolf Fella had not allowed the old medicine man to go. He had been told by the chieftain to keep a close watch on the Hillabee town. The presence of white families inside the Creek Nation so close to the village had been alarming.

The warriors moved at a good pace as they followed the familiar path to Oakfuskee, only stopping once to eat a handful of parched corn and drink from a gurgling spring. As they rounded the last bend before arriving at Oakfuskee, the town dogs announced their presence. Three large gray dogs resembling their wolf cousins, tails tucked with teeth shinning, stopped the Hillabee warriors in their tracks. Fortunately, a young warrior, following closely behind quickly called the dogs back, beckoning the Hillabee men to follow him to the town.

"Soaring Eagle, my friend, welcome," Menawa greeted, the scars from wounds he had received at the Horseshoe still visible. "I hope the dogs did not startle you. Encounters with the white man are becoming more frequent. Two suns ago, one attempted to steal food from one of the huti near the edge of the town."

"It is good to see you Menawa," Soaring Eagle said as the two men clasped arms. "We too have noticed more of the whites near Hillabee. None have tried to steal food from us," pausing he frowned, "yet. My family just saw a small family on the trail. They were joyfully singing as they traveled."

"Singing," Menawa asked, puzzled. "What words did they sing?"

"Home, Sweet Sweet home," Soaring Eagle said softly.

Anger flashed across the strong face of the man who had

fought so bravely for his people and their land. "These brazen white people think now that they can come to our homes and take them away. This will not be allowed to happen. With the new sun, we will travel to Tuckabatchee Town. We will talk with others. We will stand together. The white families can make their home in other places. This is our home, sweet home, not theirs," Menawa stopped. "Forgive me, my friend," he smiled. "I still have the fighting spirit within me. Come, let us have some of the deer that I smell roasting."

Fifty upper Tallapoosa warriors made their way down the river. They crossed the Saugahatchee on the same large stones that had dotted the creek when the women and children had been taken hostage ten seasons before. They camped under the same giant oak trees and were in awe just as the women had been when they came in sight of the sprawling town of Tuckabatchee.

Hundreds of warriors and chieftains from across the Creek Nation as well as dozens of Cherokee led by John Ridge and Elias Boudinot had gathered at Tuckabatchee Town. The last rays of the setting sun filtered across the vast area around the old council tree as the warriors talked among themselves eating the venison and turtle soup the town women had provided. The National Council would begin with the new day and the Creek men were eager to here the words of their leaders and the wisdom of the Cherokee.

Soaring Eagle and the Hillabee men spread their blankets near Menawa and the Oakfuskee people. The two leaders were just beginning to discuss what words would be spoken during the council when a young Tuckabatchee warrior approached their fire.

"Chief Menawa," the youth said, a question in his voice.

"Yes, I am Menawa. What do you wish of me?" the Chieftain asked.

"My chief, Opothle Yahola would like to speak with you. Please follow me to his home."

"I will. Soaring Eagle, I do not know what words the

Tuckabatchee leader will say. I do not know how long his talk will be. You need to sleep now. I will talk with you on the new day," Menawa said as he stiffly rose to his feet.

Soaring Eagle nodded, pulling his blanket closer around his shoulder. He was tired and quickly slipped into a deep sleep. Cold wind blew and as a full brother moon rose over the Tallapoosa River, the chilling sound filled the night. Soaring Eagle stirred as he heard the all too familiar sound. "Not the owl, not the owl," he said out loud, fearing what sadness the earie raptor's prophesy would be.

Chapter Thirteen
Tuckabatchee Council

Soaring Eagle was awakened by the early morning sounds of Tuckabatchee Town coming to life. He had listened to the cry of the owl long into the night and had only drifted back to sleep when the pre-dawn sky had begun to turn pale gray. Embarrassed, he quickly jumped up to prepare himself for the day. The call of the owl had left him with an anxious feeling about the upcoming council and the decisions that would be made. He and the other warriors from Hillabee and Oakfuskee ate the sofkee offered them and made their way to the council ground near the majestic tree that had been the site of countless councils throughout time. Watching the hundreds of Creek men as they took their places reminded Soaring Eagle of the council many seasons ago when Tecumseh had warned of what would happen to the Creek and to all the nations if they did not stand together. He had been correct, and his prediction had been so true. Soaring Eagle thought often of the events and changes that had taken place since the famed leader had given his passionate speech, tears of love for his people and their land running down his strong face.

The rapid beat of the drum signaled that the council would soon begin. Soaring Eagle smiled as he heard the drum. This was a part of their life that the white man would never take away. The drum beat was the heart beat of their soul and would continue to be far as long as the red man lived.

Tuckabatchee Chief Opothle Yahola took his place and the beat of the drum stopped. "My brothers and friends, welcome to Tuckabatchee Town," the handsome chieftain said in greeting. "Thank you for coming. We have much to talk of today and many decisions to make."

Soaring Eagle was not surprised when the chieftain began his talk by referring to the Shawnee leader Tecumseh and what if any, difference there would have been in the outcome if the Creek as well as all Indian people had stood their ground against the white man.

"Tecumseh told us what would happen if we did not listen. In the seasons since the great leader stood under this very tree, we have lost much. Hundreds of our brave, fearless warriors walked the path to the Great Spirit. Why?" The now excited warrior exclaimed, "Because many of our people joined with the white man in the battles between us. Now, some of our own people joined, yet again, in a different kind of battle. They are assisting them in taking our land and even the homes of our people."

Feeling the emotion and energy in the words of the Tuckabatchee Chieftain, many of the older warriors began yelling war cries of days and seasons gone by. The young men quickly joined in and the voices of the many warriors echoed throughout the valley of the Tallapoosa. The chilly winds and clouds of the early morning had given way to warm sunshine and the attentive warriors were eager for more of the fiery words from Opothle Yahola and others who would speak. "Our problems began in the time of our grandfathers," the Tuckabatchee Chieftain continued, "and even the time before that. The white leaders sent their traders to live among us. They brought us their useless trinkets and the metal axe. Our people liked these things. They traded the hides of the deer for things we did not need. More and more hides were required, leaving fewer deer for our people," Opothle Yahola said, realizing that his words had been spoken many times before. "When all the deer had been depleted the white man wanted something else. They wanted our land."

Animated yells from the crowd of warriors erupted again. Some of them brandishing their white-man muskets high in the air, not realizing the absurdity of their action. The Tuckabatchee leader smiled as he clutched the pearl handle of his shinny new knife. Just the day before he had purchased the knife with gold coins he had received from a man with skin as white as frost on a cold morning. He stood looking out at the mass of mostly Creek warriors. He knew that his next words would surprise them. "We, our people, have allowed this to happen. We have accepted the ways of the white man. Many of our people today live more as they do than as a Creek or Cherokee," looking directly at John Ridge and Elias Bontinot who, he knew both were wealthy and lived in fine houses and ate their food from fancy china dishes. "Yes, my brothers, we have allowed this to happen," He held his knife high in the air for all the now quiet crowd to see. "And I too am guilty. We saw how the white families live and wanted that way of life. The mistake we made was signing the first treaty and then another and another. Each taking more and more of our land. The treaty Sharp Knife Jackson forced some of our people to sign after the Horseshoe, gave nearly half of the Creek Nation to the whites. They said that was all they would take, that we could live on the land left to us without fear from more encroachment for as long as the grass grows and the rivers flow." The Chief paused again, then raising his voice in anger he continued, "They speak with tongues as forked as the fanes of the rattlesnake that slitters on the ground and waits to strike the unsuspecting. The white man will not be satisfied until they have all our land. Some of our people and even our leaders, our headmen, have fell prey to the trickery of these evil men. The promise of great sums of money have enticed our people to sell. Yes, I said sell land that does not even belong to them. Many of you were present at the Pole Cat Springs Council when it was decided that the penalty for selling our land would be death. It seems that the leader of the lower towns, William McIntosh, has not honored that decision." Sounds of disbelief and anger came from the warriors, many raising their muskets in the air again. "At the council of Indian Springs near Coweta, which was attended by mostly hand picked greedy men who were willing to sale our land, McIntosh was among the first that agreed to sale. I told him a big mistake was being made. He looked at me with contempt and signed the treaty. I and son of Big Warrior,

Tuskenah, turned away. We knew this man had just sold this own country and that McIntosh was now in great danger."

The sun was high overhead and Opothle Yahola realized his people needed to move around and have food before he continued. He was sure others would need to talk as well. The most important words of the council were yet to come. Soaring Eagle and Menawa each picked up a large piece of bread made of corn that the Tuckabatchee women now fried in a large black pot. "This is good," Soaring Eagle said as he bit into the bread, "But I would much rather have bread cooked in the ways of my mother and grandmother."

"Yes, I agree," Menawa answered. "Walk with me my friend. I have words to say before the council continues." The two leaders walked away from the clamor of the Creek warriors who were all engaged in conversation about the words spoken in council, all of them curious about the importance of what would be said when the council resumed. "Soaring Eagle," Menawa said softly when they were out of the hearing range of the others. "I have received orders from Opothle Yahola. I have been charged to go to the Chattahoochee," the battle-scared warrior paused briefly, his eyes searching those of Soaring Eagle, "to carry out the death penalty on the one who has sold out our people and our land. I was told to take the life of McIntosh. I will need you and the brave warriors of the Oakfuskee and the Hillabee to accompany me. This will be a dangerous action and could result in serious retaliation for our people," he paused again, "But it must be done. We have no choice if we continue to keep our land."

Soaring Eagle nodded, remembering the visit of the owl the night before. He experienced a sick feeling deep in the pit of his stomach, one that was quickly replaced by an equally deep feeling of honor. Menawa was right, this had to be done. The two chieftains returned to the council ground just as the drum beat signaled that the council would resume. Opothle Yahola again took his place, looking out over the crowd of warriors. "I hope each of you are comfortable now and are ready to continue. Words that need to be said will be many as any who wishes may speak," the respected leader announced.

As predicted, the council continued with many of the leaders speaking, using the same strong heart-felt words as Opothle Yahola had. A stand must be made now against the white man if the Creek and others of the red race are to survive.

    The sun set, casting its orange glow in the western sky and the fire light begin to twinkle over Tuckabatchee. Opolthle Yahola's voice was loud and strong as he said the words the crowd had waited to hear. In the time of planting, Menawa will lead his strongest and bravest warriors to the Chattahoochee. The death penalty will be carried out. McIntosh must die.

Chapter Fourteen
Eyes That See Me

Little Flower and Sun Flower Woman listened closely as Soaring Eagle told them of the events of the Tuckabatchee Council. He waited until last to tell them that he, Fox Slayer and Horse Stealer would be going with Menawa and other warriors from Hillabee on the mission to carry out the penalty that had been proclaimed. Having experienced the horror of the Horseshoe and the difficult, frightening time since, neither woman was surprised. Little Flower, a lump forming in her throat and tears threatening to fall from her beautiful sad eyes, tried to compose herself. She was proud of her husband and realized that he certainly would be required to go to Coweta.

"Yes, my husband. When will this mission take place?" Little Flower asked in a small voice.

"My son, while we realize you must go," trying to be calm, Sun Flower Woman began. "We will fear for your safety and that of my grandson and the husband of my granddaughter."

"My wife and my mother," Soaring Eagle answered gravely. "Since the time before the grandfathers, the warrior has had the responsibility to do what is best for our people. This must be done. I must go."

Taking the hands of his wife, Soaring Eagle continued, "when brother moon is next big and bright in the sky, we will go to Acorn Bluff on the Chattahoochee. The home of the traitor of our people, William McIntosh. Tell no one of this. It is possible that some who live among us would alert him. One of the daughters of Trader Grierson married a son of McIntosh," pausing, he tenderly brushed the tears from the face of this wife. "We will talk no more of this. Come, let us go to the huti of Little Deer. I have gifts for my family from the Tuckabatchee Chief, Opothle Yahola. Do not forget, my words go no farther."

Soaring Eagle smiled as his young daughter jumped into

his arms. "My father, I am happy to see you," Morning Star exclaimed. "I did not know you were back from your trip."

"Yes, my little one," Soaring Eagle answered the child, then looking at his older daughter, surprised to see that her stomach had grown so in the few suns he had been gone. "And Little Deer, I see that my grandson will soon arrive. It is good that the number of our people continues to grow."

Smiling at her father, Little Deer answered, "My father, it is good that you have safely returned. I hope your trip was pleasant as you traveled down the Tallapoosa and that the council was a success. Yes, my time will be soon. I know my son will be strong and brave just like his grandfather," pausing, the happy young woman continued as she looked at Horse Stealer, "and his father."

"My father, what is in your pouch? It looks so big and fat," Morning Star asked as she gingerly touched the brown bag hanging from her father's shoulder.

"Careful, Little one," Soaring Eagle answered, laughing at the child. "It may have teeth and could bite you." Quickly removing her hand from the bag, Morning Star jumped back. "Chief Opothle Yahola sends gifts to my wife and daughter and for you also Sun Flower Woman. That is the reason for the size of my pouch," Soaring Eagle said as a big smile covered the face of his young daughter. He slowly pulled out a package wrapped in brown paper, bright red and blue showing around the edges.

"What manner of wrapping is this," Sun Flower Woman asked. "I have not seen this before."

Soaring Eagle smiled again, "It is paper like the white man uses for his books, but it is thicker and brown." He handed a package to each of the women, then gave Morning Star an oddly-shaped one.

The little girl squealed in delight as she unwrapped her package and then just as quickly screamed in fear as a baby doll fell to the ground. "My father, it has eyes. It is looking at me," Morning Star cried out, hiding her face in the open arms of her grandmother.

"Little one, please do not be afraid," Soaring Eagle said, surprised at her reaction. "It is only a doll. It cannot harm you."

"My son," Sun Flower Woman began. "The child has never seen the doll of the white children," she paused, "and I have not either. It is frightening. Did you forget that the face of the Creek doll has no eyes."

The family of Soaring Eagle watched in silence as Morning Star, with a defiant look, picked up the doll. "My mother, may I use your scissors?"

Without questioning her daughter, Little Flower pulled trade scissors from her skirt band and gave them to the child. "My father, I will not fear this doll and I will not fear the white people," she said as she clipped the black button eyes from the doll. "Now, I have a doll that is both Creek and white," the child said as she happily cradled the doll in her arms.

The family was stunned by the words of the child. Sun Flower Woman was the first to speak as she slid the bright red shawl from the paper wrap. "My granddaughter has much wisdom for one so young. She seems to understand the change that has taken place with our people. We now live as both red and white," she smiled as she spread the shawl over her shoulders. "I too will change this. What is it called?" she asked, looking at Soaring Eagle.

"A shawl, my mother, it is called by the white women," Soaring Eagle answered. "It is much liked by them."

"I will add some of my white beads to the edge and this shawl will keep me warm when the wind blows cold," the wise older woman replied. "I too will not fear the white man and I will remain a woman of the Wind Clan for as long as my eyes see the new day."

Chapter Fifteen
Instructions for the Law Menders

Soaring Eagle held Little Flower close, tenderly kissing her. He lifted her face looking into her tear-filled eyes, both remembering the time before the Horseshoe. "My Flower, please do not cry. I am not going into battle this time. I will return safely to you," Soaring Eagle promised, releasing his wife and turning to fill his pouch with the items he would need for the trip down the Tallapoosa and from there over to the Chattahoochee. He could not bare to see the pain and fear so evident in her sad, beautiful face.

"I realize my Eagle," Little Flower replied softly, wiping the tears from her cheeks. "There is much danger in your mission. I cannot control the fear that I feel."

"I do not know how long the trip will take. I need for you to be alert and be watchful. The white people continue to move closer to our towns. If there is any problem, go to Wolf Fella. He may be old now and slow, but he will know what to do. Remember how much I love you and that I will return," Soaring Eagle said, gently touching her cheek then walking out the door of the cabin, the soft light of the full moon shinning on his strong face.

The law menders, as the group would be known, silently made their way down the river. This was the second time in as many moons and their pace was quick and sure. Menawa and his warriors were waiting and before the morning sun had risen over the east bank, the now larger group had left Oakfuskee Town. They would walk until darkness again covered the sky, stopping only for a brief rest and to eat dried corn. After sleeping for a short time, the warriors were again on the move and reached the town of Tuckabatchee as the evening sun dipped below the western horizon. The up-river warriors, as always, when visiting the sprawling town, were in awe of the bustle and activity. Most of them preferring the quiet peace of their towns. Opothle Yahola had guards posted, watching for his comrade's arrival and they were quickly taken to his home.

"My friends," the Tuckabatchee Chieftain said in greeting. "It is good to see you again. I hope your trip down the Tallapoosa was good. Our women have prepared food. You will need to eat and then rest. Before the sun shows her face on the new day, your mission will begin." Looking at Menawa and Soaring Eagle, the respected chieftain continued, "I need to speak to the two of you. I have instructions from members of the National Council on how this deed must be carried out."

The up-river leaders nodded and followed Opothle Yahola inside his home. Both men noticed the many items of the white man mixed with traditional ones of their people. It was obvious that this man had accumulated much wealth and lived very comfortably.

"Please sit down," he said, pointing to two straight-backed chairs, the bottoms covered with plush crimson cushions. Noticing the discomfort of the warriors, the Tuckabatchee Chieftain smiled. "Those belong to my wife. I do not sit on them either. Come, follow me to a place that is more suited for the warriors of our people."

Menawa and Soaring Eagle followed Opothle Yahola to a smaller room that resembled their own homes. Both men sat on the small couch covered by a traditional Creek blanket. "My chief," Menawa began, "We are ready to hear our orders."

The Tuckabatchee Chieftain sat down opposite the leader, his face now serious. "My brothers, the two of you have been selected to lead this mission. There will be danger. The brave warriors from your towns joined with the Tuckabatchee will be a considerable number, possibly as many as one-hundred, seventy-five. This number will make the time of travel longer. Still your arrival near Acorn Bluff will take three or four suns. The plantation of the White Warrior is large, and he has many black men to do his work. His home is in the big curve of the

Chattahoochee and from a distance appears to be on the other side of the river. You must take the time to watch the activities. Do not allow your presence to be known. The White Warrior is aware of his death sentence. He does not know when it will happen. I have received word that he is in preparation for a trip to the west," Opothle Yahola paused, "to look at land for his new home. This trip will not be allowed to happen. The head man of Coweta and two sons-in-law of McIntosh, Sam and Ben Hawkins, who also signed the treaty to give our land to the white man, they too will not live. Do not harm the wives or young children of McIntosh. We are not killers of women and babies. Also, no white person will be killed. This deed must be done deliberately and swiftly. Before the first streaks of the morning sun shines in the sky, the White Warrior and the others will be punished for the deed they have done to all our people. May the Great Spirit guide you and keep you free from harm."

Chapter Sixteen
Penalty of Death

Heavy clouds hung low over the Tallapoosa and rain began to fall as the law menders began their journey. The rain continued, and the small streams became large, making travel difficult. A few of the Creek warriors carried small skin boats used for crossing streams. The others, being excellent swimmers, swam across the rapidly rising water with no fear. Despite the inclement weather, the large entourage of warriors reached the area of Locks Chau Talofa or Acorn Buff, the magnificent home of William McIntosh, before nightfall of the third day. The new leaves of the giant hardwood trees and thick river cane that lined the Chattahoochee, hid the presence of the cold and wet warriors. Still, no fires would be made as the warriors watched the big home and the many out houses that surrounded it. Soaring Eagle and Menawa sat a short distance from the others discussing the magnitude of their mission. Suddenly, two men on horses appeared on a trail near the river. The men were McIntosh and Sam Hawkins. McIntosh continued to ride in the direction of the house and Hawkins turned onto the western trail that led back to the Tallapoosa, both unaware that they were being watched. The men were easy targets, but this was not the time. Following instructions from the National Council, the deed would be carried out before dawn of the next new day and in view of the families of the doomed men.

   The warriors were instructed to gather pine kindling and arrange in bundles. The law menders waited patiently. First one whippoorwill and then another and another began their symphony of calls. Now was the time. Several warriors slipped out of hiding, placing the pine kindling around the house where McIntosh slept. The signal was given. Bright flames slowly crept up the wall of the house.

"McIntosh, McIntosh," one of the Creek warriors called out. "We are here! You were warned! You will sell no more of the land that belongs to our people."

Menawa stepped forward, indicating for his warriors to hold their words. "General McIntosh," he began, his voice strong and clear. "We have been sent by the National Council of our nation. You know of the death penalty that hangs over your head. Send your wives and small children out of the house. We do not want them to be injured for the deed that you have done," Menawa paused, "And if you have guest that are white, they too will not be harmed."

More of the out buildings were torched, the flames quickly spreading up the sides of the wooden structures. Warrior yells and screams of panic filled the pre-dawn air. The scene was one of pandemonium as men of all colors, red, black and white fled for safety from both the consuming flames and the shots from the muskets of the animated warriors. Soaring Eagle watched as the figures of two women and their children ran from the burning house, screaming for their husband to follow. The brave warrior quickly pulled them to safety.

McIntosh stood in an upstairs window firing down on the warriors below. As the raging fire began to lick its way up the staircase, the White Warrior rushed past the flames to the entrance of what had been his grand home. He showed no fear as the bullets from the warrior's muskets pelted his body. After being pulled outside, he looked defiantly at the warriors surrounding him. Menawa towered over the now destitute man and quickly performed the deed he had been sent to do, plunging his knife deep into the heart of the man who had sold out his own people. As in times of old, the agitated warriors then rushed to complete the task. More shots were fired into the body of McIntosh, he was then scalped.

Menawa and Soaring Eagle walked away as their warriors killed the cattle and hogs that had belonged to McIntosh. Some of the men taking clothing and jewelry that had belonged to the wives of McIntosh and money from the pockets of the dead man. This was not necessary and were not the actions the law menders had been sent to do. Menawa watched in sadness as some of his men acted more like the savages they were accused of being by the white man, than the honorable warriors he had hoped they would be.

It was over. The death penalty had been accomplished. General McIntosh, the White Warrior and several other men who had signed the white man's paper no longer lived. They would sign no more treaties that gave the land of the Creek people to the greedy white race.

Chapter Seventeen
The Deed Is Done

Allowing only a brief time for the warriors to enjoy what they had thought of as a victory, Menawa called them together, noticing that some of them had received minor injuries during the attack. "My brothers, we have done the deed we were asked to do. We will return now to the Tallapoosa. We will waste no time in returning home. What we have done will not bring an end to our troubles. The white man is not satisfied with the land that he has already taken from our people. He wants all of the land that belongs to us," Menawa paused, looking out at the warriors, he sadly continued. "I hope that our deed will allow the Creek people time to regroup and stand together. Go to you homes. Plant your corn and beans. Enjoy the hunt, the ball games and ceremonies. Spend time with your woman. Teach your children the way of our people. My brothers, I fear that we will continue to lose the ways of the grandmothers and they will be forever gone. Thank each of you for assisting me with this mission. Go now." The Oakfuskee Chieftain turned away, some saying that he wiped a tear from his strong face.

The Tuckabatchee, Oakfuskee and Hillabee warriors left the partially burned plantation of the White Warrior. The fine big house and out buildings still smoldering. Many of the slaves were taken and one of the Okfuskee warriors had the reddish hair of McIntosh dangling from his belt. This trophy would be hung from a scalp pole in the square ground when he returned home.

****

The young Coweta warrior had watched in disbelief and fear as the big house slowly went up in flames. His heart beat quickened when he heard the yells and musket fire from who he knew were Creek warriors. "The law menders," he said to himself. "Badger said they would come. I must hurry back home and tell him. He will know what to do." The young warrior had ventured far up the Chattahoochee in search of an elusive wild turkey. The morning sun had not yet showed itself and he knew he must waste no time if he were to make it back home before darkness again covered the sky.

The young warrior arrived back in Coweta as the town people were preparing their evening meal. He went quickly to the home of Badger who had just sat down to eat his rabbit stew and bread. "Badger, Badger," the youth called out. "They have come, the law menders have come."

"Acorn Bluff," Badger questioned, knowing the young man had been upriver. He had received word from the Tallapoosa Towns and knew the National Council would tolerate no more land sales. The Coweta leader understood, realizing that each treaty took more and more land from his people. He had warned the White Warrior, telling him that he would die if the signed the treaty of Indian Springs. McIntosh had not listened, greed for the money of the white man was too strong.

Badger picked up his musket and pouch. He knew he must go up river to Acorn Bluff. He was not sure what he would do to help. He did not want the innocent to be harmed and he also realized that the white militia and landowners would soon converge on the Bluff. The law menders should leave the area quickly, or they too would suffer.

Guided by the moonlight, the Coweta warrior made good time using the northern path that led to the plantation home of McIntosh. He had stopped to drink from a bubbling spring that ran from the hillside. As he stood to resume his journey, he heard the loud blast of a musket and felt instant pain, the blood running down his arm. He fell forward and was quickly surrounded by Creek warriors.

The law menders, thinking it best to return to the Tallapoosa as quickly as possible had decided to take the shortest route, the same route Badger had taken. Hearing the musket shot, Soaring Eagle and Menawa immediately ran to see what had happened. Parting the group of warriors, Soaring Eagle gasped as he recognized his old friend and adversary. "Badger," he shouted as he pulled the turban from his own head and wrapped it around the gushing wound.

"Soaring Eagle," the injured man said softly as he grimaced in pain. "I had hoped to see you again," he said with a fleeting smile, "I did not know I would need to be shot to do so."

"Save your words, my brother," Soaring Eagle answered, "Until I see how serious your injury is."

Menawa looked at the group of warriors and asked, "Why did you shoot this man before you knew of his intentions?"

"We saw him lurking in the bushes. I thought that he was one of the McIntosh people," the spokesman for the group answered, obviously the warrior who had fired the musket. Hoping to rectify the deed, he added, "I could have shot him through the heart instead of his arm." Looking at Badger the warrior said in an attempted apology, "My brother, I will now do what I can to help the situation."

Soaring Eagle lifted the make-shift tunicate from Badger's arm and tenderly examined the wound. "Fortunately, my brother, it is a flesh wound. The ball went completely through your arm. You will have pain for a few suns, but you will recover."

The warriors seemed to be in a hurry to continue on their way, nervously looked back up the moonlit path. In sudden realization, Badger smiled and asked, "are you the law menders?"

Menawa nodded, he and Badger had never met eye to eye, both having heard of the other's bravery and honor. "Badger, I am happy that your injury is not serious, and you are correct, the deed is done. The white leaders and soldiers will come to Acorn Bluff, but they will not follow us back to the Tallapoosa. They were aware of the death penalty proclaimed by the National Council and that it would be acted upon." The Tallapoosa Chieftain paused, "What of you, what is your stand?"

"Menawa, my chief," the injured man began, gingerly touching his arm. "I have lived most of my life in the Town of Coweta. I have seen the progress our people have made in their association with the white race. I have seen also, the great loss. Our people no longer retain the ways of our ancestors and," Badger paused, "We no longer have our land. I have many times had talks with the White Warrior, his sons and others of the treaty party, but to no avail. That is my stand."

"Badger, you and your family should return with us to the Tallapoosa," Soaring Eagle said, as he looked back up the path. "You will no longer be safe here."

"You are correct, Soaring Eagle, "the Coweta leader answered. "I will go with you. I have no family."

"No family," Soaring Eagle questioned, frowning slightly. "Have you never taken a wife," remembering the time after the Horseshoe when Badger saved his family from certain death by bringing them to Coweta. He also remembered that this man had fallen deeply in love with his wife, Little Flower.

Badger smiled, remembering Little Flower. "I took a wife after you and your family returned home. She left with a white trader with long red hair on his face." Becoming serious, Badger continued, "Do not fear my brother, I will love your wife only as a sister." Feeling a slight flutter in his heart, he thought to himself, "I hope."

Chapter Eighteen
Return to the Tallapoosa

Soaring Eagle and Badger quickly made the trip to Coweta while Menawa led the others back to the Tallapoosa. The mother of Badger had succumbed to one of the fevers of the white man during the cold season. He indeed had no family remaining in his town. He picked up his few belongings from his cabin and bid his friends farewell. They already knew he would need to leave. The two warriors walked in silence as they rushed to rejoin the other Hillabee and Oakfuskee warriors.

As they rounded the bend that lead to the Tallapoosa path, the two men stopped as they heard shouts and then the blast of muskets being fired. Two Creek men, dressed in the clothing of the white man, lay on the ground, both apparently had breathed their last. One of the Hillabee warriors looked at Soaring Eagle and explained, "We were ambushed by these men. We took care of them."

"They signed the treaty," Badger said, looking at the men. Both are relatives of McIntosh."

"Good," Soaring Eagle answered, "Let us continue on to the Tallapoosa."

The journey was uneventful, and in four days, the law menders saw the smoke coming from the rock and clay chimney of the cabins. Badger had listened with much interest and joy as Soaring Eagle had told him of his family. Not only had the Coweta warrior loved the wife of Soaring Eagle, he had become enraptured with the delightful little girl who showed no fear and her more serious twin brother that had allowed his sister to think that she was the best shot and could always out do him. Badger had often wondered what had happened to the little family that he had been ready to make his own and of his friend, Horse Stealer. The brave young warrior who always seemed to make trouble for himself, had fled with the family to the Tallapoosa avoiding certain hanging when Soaring Eagle had returned from the dead to reclaim his family. Badger had been surprised when Soaring Eagle had told him of the marriage between Horse Stealer and Little Deer. Surely the child was much too young to become a wife. Smiling at Badger, Soaring Eagle had reminded him that it had been more than ten cold seasons since he had seen Little Deer and that she certainly was no longer a child as she would very soon have a child of her own. Soaring Eagle added that Horse Stealer and Fox Slayer, as he was called now, had made the journey from Hillabee to Tuckabatchee, but Chief Menawa had asked the two warriors to take word of the upcoming deed to other leaders in the Creek Nation. One more thing Soaring Eagle added, Little Flower and I do have a young daughter, Morning Star. She has seen four warm seasons. She looks like her mother and has the ways of her older sister.

You are a fortunate man Soaring Eagle, Badger had told him, trying to hide the envy he had felt, realizing that he still had strong forbidden feelings for the wife of this man. What of Sun Flower Woman he had asked, hoping that his thoughts were not apparent to Soaring Eagle. She has become one of the Beloved Women he had answered. She is strong and has much wisdom. Her strength has helped guide our people, keeping us together.

Barking dogs announced the arrival of the returning warriors. The little girl playing with a doll with no eyes had anticipated the homecoming of her father. She gathered up the strange doll and ran to greet the Hillabee warriors. "My father, my father," she excitedly yelled as she ran to him.

"Morning Star, my little one," Soaring Eagle said," dropping his pouch and bending to pick the child up, swinging her high in the air. The Hillabee warriors smiled as they watched their leader and the little girl, still not fully understanding this show of affection. This was Soaring Eagle, he was, after all, different. Some of them realized that this was what made him such a good leader. He loved his family and his people.

Badger heard her voice before he saw her, his heart immediately beating faster. "Soaring Eagle, oh Soaring Eagle," Little Flower exclaimed as she also ran to greet the man who was her husband.

Putting his daughter down, he turned to his wife, holding her close. "My flower," Soaring Eagle whispered softly. "My little flower." He slowly released his wife, realizing that his warriors were still watching. He then remembered that Badger was there also. "Little Flower, I have brought an old friend," pausing, hoping that he was just an old friend, "back from Coweta."

Little Flower stood frozen as she looked at him. "Badger," she said, regaining her composure. "You have been hurt. Come let me see to your injury."

Badger looked at the still shocked woman who seemed even more beautiful now. Her eyes suddenly filling with sadness. "Why are you here," she asked as she softly touched his swollen arm.

Wishing that he had been the one she had rushed to greet, he smiled. "It is good to see you, Little Flower. It was well-known that I opposed the treaty signed by McIntosh. Soaring Eagle thought it best that I return with him."

Soaring Eagle watched as Badger gazed intently at his wife. She returned his look and for a fleeting moment, all three knew that if he had not survived the Horseshoe, Little Flower would belong to the Coweta warrior.

Little Deer, resting inside her cabin had heard a familiar voice from the past. "Badger," she screamed, holding her large stomach as she tried to run to him. "I did not think I would see you again."

Not hesitating, Badger opened his arms and held the young woman that he still thought of as a little girl. "Little Deer, Little Deer," the emotional warrior exclaimed as a tear escaped from his eye. "You are no longer that mischievous child that I remember you being."

"No, Badger," Little Deer replied, wiping tears from her own eyes. "I am not and as you can see, I will soon have a child of my own."

Watching the scene before him, Soaring Eagle could not prevent the feeling of jealousy that washed over him. Had he made a mistake bringing Badger to his home, this man who had made such an impression on his family?

The dogs began barking again, but quickly became silent when they recognized Fox Slayer and Horse Stealer who had returned from their journey to other parts of the Creek Nation. They had joined Sun Flower Woman on the path as she returned from gathering herbs for her medicine. The reunion continued when the warriors realized that the visitor was Badger. Both men going immediately to him. "Badger, it is good to see you," Horse Stealer said, grasping the older man's arm in the manner of a mature warrior.

Fox Slayer, resisting the urge to hug the man followed the actions of his friend. "Badger," the young warrior asked, "Why are you here?" Giving the same response he had given earlier, the warriors then gathered to talk of the events that had transpired, asking the women to prepare food for them.

Little Flower and her daughters and mother quickly did as they were asked, cheerfully talking about the arrival of Badger. "My mother," the little voice of Morning Star interrupted. "Who is this man? Why is he here? How long will he stay and why are all of you so happy to see him?"

"My, my, child, you certainly have many questions," Sun Flower Woman answered, laughing at her granddaughter, recalling the feelings she knew Badger had for Little Flower. "Well, my daughter," Little Flower began, "You have heard of the terrible time after the Horseshoe." The little girl nodded. "We were taken far away to another town."

"The one on the river called Flowered Rocks," Morning Star inquired?

"Yes, that is right," Little Flower continued. "This man, called Badger, took us there and he was very good to us and kept us from harm. Now for his own safety, your father has brought him here."

"That is good my mother. Why does my father look so sad?" the little girl asked as if she knew there was more than she was being told.

Sun Flower Woman looked at her daughter and then answered her granddaughter, "My Star, your father is tired from his journey. Your mother will make him happy again. Let us go now and take food to our family."

After the warriors had finished eating and talking about the feat that had been accomplished, each was ready to retire to their own home. Before going to the cabin that had been assigned to him, the Coweta warrior turned to Soaring Eagle. "My brother, may I have words with you in private before we sleep?" The Hillabee Chieftain nodded and sat back down by the dying fire. "My friend," Badger began, "I need to tell you what I feel in my heart. I was happy to see your wife," he paused, "and your son and daughter. I have missed them, all of them. I must not lie to you. When I looked at Little Flower, I wished that she was my wife." Seeing the look of anger that flashed across the other man's face, he continued. "She is not. She is the wife of Soaring Eagle. My brother, I will protect her from the harm of any man and with the honor of all my people, I will never attempt to take her from you." Badger stopped and smiled at the warrior sitting across from him, "She would never allow that, her love for you is strong and true. I will, if you are not comfortable with me being here, go to the town of Oakfuskee with the new day. That is all I have to say."

Both men rose, looking deeply into the eyes of the other. Soaring Eagle nodded, slowly grasping the good arm of Badger. "I trust you and I know of the love you have for my Little Flower. You may stay at Hillabee," Soaring Eagle continued, his voice becoming cold. "My brother, if the words you have said to me are untrue, then you will die." As if the two men were planning a hunting trip, the mood of Soaring Eagle quickly changed. "My brother, rest well, with the new sun our people will begin planning for the hard times to come." As the two warriors parted, one going to an empty cabin and the other to the warm comforting arms of his wife, the familiar and chilling cry of the owl filled the silent town. Both men paused, looking at each other. "May the Great Spirit guide us and keep us from harm," Soaring Eagle softly said.

Part Two
Hard Times to Come
May 1830

Chapter Nineteen
Owl of Wood

Morning Star turned to see why Little Coyote was so far behind. The child of Little Flower and Soaring Eagle had seen ten summers and had spent much of her time during the last five seasons looking after the son of her older sister, Little Deer. The two were going across the old bridge that spanned White Oak Creek to the almost abandoned farm of trader Robert Grierson. Only a few of his people remained on what once had been a thriving complex near the Hillabee Town. Grierson had died several seasons since and many of his large family had also died or had already moved to the new land called Indian Territory. Old Sinnugee, his wife, and several of her grandchildren still lived on the farm that was only a shadow of what it had once been. Morning Star had gone with her mother many times to visit the aging woman and enjoyed hearing her tell stories of what had happened long ago. When she had gotten excited, the old woman would speak in a different tongue that Little Flower had explained was the talk of the Shawnee. The little girl hoped that she would talk that way today. What was Little Coyote doing that was taking so long she wondered, not seeing the child that was in her care.

"Coyote, Little Coyote," Morning Star called out. "Where are you?" Fear gripped her when she saw the little boy, a bright trickle of red running down his arm. "Little Coyote, what has happened?"

"Not hurt bad," the child said as the tears began to slide down his brown face. "I fall down on rocks," he smiled. "Try to catch fish with my hands to give grandmother. See?" He smiled again, holding up a small sun bream that flipped back and forth in his hand.

Smiling back at the little boy, after she quickly examined his arm and making sure that he was indeed not badly injured, Morning Star picked up a forked stick and placed it through the mouth of the fish. "Now, hold this stick and your fish will not jump out of your hand," in her motherly tone, Morning Star continued. "Now, let me see your hurt arm again. Looking up and down the bank of the little stream and seeing what she needed to stop the bleeding, the older child found and then quickly placed bear grass on the arm of Little Coyote. "I think we are ready to continue on our way, we cannot stay long. My sister, your mother, will worry if we do not return home before the sun goes behind the big hill."

The old Creek woman who was indeed mixed with the blood of the Shawnee, smiled and held out her arms to the children she loved seeing and the child Morning Star who reminded her so much of her spirited mother.

"Morning Star and Little Coyote," she exclaimed. "It is good that you have come to see me this day."

"Grandmother Sinnugee," the child called out. "I have brought you a fish. You can eat it for your next meal."

"Oh Coyote, that is just what I would like to eat. Will you prepare the fish for me, so I can cook it?" Seeing the blood that had dried on his arm, Sinnugee continued. "What happened to your arm?"

"I fall," Little Coyote said timidly, not wanting the woman to know the entire story. "Star make it better," he finished as he looked adoringly at his aunt.

"Let me see," the older woman ordered as she raised his arm. She nodded approvingly, thinking that Morning Star was learning the ways of the Creek women. "It will turn the color of the nighttime sky and will be sore. "Star," she said, looking at the little girl. "I am proud that you knew what to do."

Morning Star smiled at Sinnugee. "My mother and grandmother and you too grandmother Sinnugee, teach me the old ways of our people. I know that this is good."

Sinnugee smiled again and patted the head of the little girl, her beautiful hair shinning in the sunlight.

"Grandmother Sinnugee," Little Coyote said, tugging on her apron. "I go get fish ready for you to cook."

"That is good, Coyote," the old woman said. "When you finish come inside. I have fresh bread made from corn and I will pour honey on the top for you."

The little boy screamed in delight as he ran to the back side of her small cabin that had once served as the home of one of her husband's slaves. "Morning Star, come. I have something special for you too," Sinnugee said, opening the door for the child, as sunlight filtered in through the open windows, dancing on the brightly colored rugs that she had made. The cabin was filled with many traditional items of the Creek people. Sinnugee now used very few of the white trade goods that had filled her home in the past.

Picking up a basket that she had made from river cane, the older woman walked over to Morning Star and removed a colorful pouch decorated with rows of tiny white beads. "This is for you, my little star. I made this pouch for you to carry your doll, preventing it from becoming soiled."

"Oh, grandmother Sinnugee," the little girl exclaimed as she touched the doll that hung from her belt. She had been afraid of it when her father Soaring Eagle had given her the doll of a white child many seasons before. With simple knowledge of a child she had removed the eyes that had frightened her and had proclaimed the doll as being both Indian and white. Sun Flower Woman had showed her granddaughter how to mend the frayed ends, keeping the doll pretty and neat.

"Now you can keep your doll in the pouch," Sinnugee said as she tied the strings of the pouch to the little girl's belt. "I have something else for you," the woman said, reaching deep into the basket. Morning Star gasped when she saw the little wooden owl in Sinnugee's hand.

"Owl!" The little girl screamed, backing up in obvious fear. "Grandmother Sinnugee, why have you given me an owl? You know what that means to us."

"Do not be afraid, Morning Star, Sinnugee consoled. "Let me explain why I want to give you this. I know to our people the owl is a sign of bad things to happen. To me the owl is warning us to get ready and prepare for what is ahead. Without the warning our people would suffer more. He is our friend," she paused, "do you understand now?"

Morning Star took the little owl from Sinnugee's hand, the piercing eyes seeming to look directly at her. Suddenly a ray of sunlight danced on the wooden figure. To the child the owl then came to life and she understood what had been told her. "Yes, I understand. I know the owl does not bring us bad things. It has come to warn us of those things."

Sinnugee smiled, "Morning Star, you are wise beyond your age. You will lead our people and become a beloved woman.

Shadows had begun to fall when the children left the home of old Sinnugee. Morning Star took the hand of Little Coyote as they crossed over the bridge that led to the path back to Hillabee Town. She touched the pouch that held her gift from Sinnugee when they heard the sad cry of the owl and she was not afraid.

Chapter Twenty
Grave Words from Sharp Knife

The morning routine of the village was disturbed the following day with the return of the son of Soaring Eagle and Little Flower. Fox Slayer and several of the Hillabee warriors had made the down-river trip for the grand council held at Tuckabatchee Town. Fox Slayer told his father that he had grave news to relay to his people and asked if the town crier could call everyone to the square ground. Over the years, much change had occurred, things were different and fewer people now lived at Hillabee. With small fields closer to the town the women and their young children quickly gathered around the edge of the square ground, the men already there with their pipes in hand. The group of Hillabee people waited quietly and patiently while Fox Slayer spoke with Soaring Eagle. Retaining the old way of beginning any council meeting, even one unexpectedly called, a single beat of the drum indicated that talk would now begin. Soaring Eagle walked to the center of the square ground and as he always did, quietly looked at all his people before beginning.

"My brothers, friends, family and all of the Hillabee people, my son Fox Slayer and other warriors of our town have just returned from Tuckabatchee. He has disturbing news that he will now tell you."

Fox Slayer, tall and strikingly handsome stood, his demeanor indicating strength and wisdom. He had not yet taken a wife, much to the disappointment of many Hillabee maidens. His father watched with pride as his son followed the same routine that he had done, slowly looking at the people before him.

"My Hillabee family," he began slowly but loud and distinct. "As my father, and chief of our town has said, we have just returned from Tuckabatchee Town," the warrior paused again, a fleeting look of sadness covered his strong face. "Many times, I have awakened from a deep sleep, my body covered with moisture with visions vivid in my mind of the sounds of that day over fifteen cold seasons ago, the day of the Horseshoe. The day when so many of our brave warriors breathed their last and the day that the ways of our people were forever changed. We have seen the white people continue to move closer and closer to us, treaty after treaty allowing this to happen. The treaty of Indian Springs, the Treaty of Washington and Fort Mitchell, each one taking more of our land and even our homes." The voice of the strong warrior becoming louder, his fist clinched as he continued. "Now, my people, the Great White Father in Washington, Sharp Knife Jackson…" many in the crowd jeered at the mention of the name of the man who had created such havoc and sadness for the Creek Nation. "My people, this man has signed papers that will not only take away our land, but also remove us from it."

The voice of Fox Slayer was drowned out by the yells and shouts of the Hillabee people. Holding up his hand to silence them, he continued. "Jackson has said that all Indian people will be removed from their home, the land of their grandfathers, to a different land across the big river, to a place called Indian Territory. This will happen over the next few years. He has said, all will go."

The shocked Hillabee stood in silence, some of the women pulling their children near them as tears fell from dark eyes that had already seen much change and sadness. The old men, several holding on to carved canes for support, their wrinkled faces set in a look of painful sorrow, stared upward toward the heavens as if asking the Great Spirit why this was happening. The younger warriors, most of which had lost their father or grandfather at the Horseshoe, looked defiantly at Fox Slayer.

"My father should have killed him, this man called Sharp Knife Jackson," one of the warriors yelled. "He and the despised white race of people have done enough to us. Why can they not just leave us alone?"

"Yes, why did they want to take everything from us," another asked, his voice rising in anger. "We should fight the whites and run them from our land."

One of the older warriors who had been at the Horseshoe and had suffered from wounds that still bothered him quietly said, "We have fought them, and we were defeated. We do not have warriors to fight again. The grandfathers of many seasons ago told of the white race of people and their great numbers. They told of how these people would come and take the deer we needed to survive and then they would take our land to make it their own. This has happened. What can we do?"

The Hillabee people were again silent, each thinking of the words that had been spoken. Fox Slayer looked at Soaring Eagle and with an encouraging look from his father he continued. "My people, it is my understanding that this," he paused, "removal of our people will not be immediate. This will take time. Sharp Knife Jackson and the people who surround him do not know what to do with us. The Hillabee people will continue to plant our corn and celebrate the ceremony of renewal. We will ask the Great Spirit to guide and protect us."

Fox Slayer stepped aside, and his father faced his people again. "My people," he said, "we are survivors. As my son has spoken, we will continue to live our life as we know it for as long as we can. Return to the activities of this day."
As the Hillabee returned to their routine, they heard the distant call of the owl, the sound chilling and sober once again.

Chapter Twenty-One
Wisdom of a Child

Soaring Eagle and his family returned to their cabin. Badger too had been asked to come. The men sat in silence, the smoke from their pipes encircling their heads. Fox Slayer paced from one side of the cabin to the other. It was obvious that the warrior wanted his family to be together and he had more words to say to them.

Little Flower broke the silence as she sat down by her husband. "The owl, will it ever leave us? Each time we hear its cry, we have more sad times and sorrow." The beautiful but now more mature woman said softly as Little Coyote sat down at the feet of his grandmother.

Morning Star also sat down by her mother and slowly removed her gift from the new pouch Sinnugee had given her. Her family looked in disbelief at the small owl figure with the glass eyes shining eerily in the child's hand.

"Morning Star," Little Flower said, disapprovingly, "where did you get that?"

"From Sinnugee," the little girl said softly. "She made this pouch for my doll as well as the new owl. Mother, please let me keep it."

"Why would you want to keep it?" Little Flower asked. "You know what the owl means to us."

"Yes, my mother, I do," Morning Star said as she brushed away tears that threatened to run down her cheek. "Please, may I tell you what grandmother Sinnugee said about the owl and his cry?"

"Let the child explain," Sun Flower Woman said from the other side of the cabin.

Little Flower nodded. "Tell us Morning Star why you want to keep this, this symbol of sadness."

Suddenly feeling shy, an emotion uncommon for the little girl, Morning Star slowly began. "Grandmother Sinnugee said that the owl did not bring to us the bad, sad times, but was warning us so that we could prepare for them. She said that the owl is our friend and not to be feared," the child, holding up the small figure, paused and looked at her family. "I want to keep the owl and the doll," looking at Soaring Eagle, "that my father gave me. Together they will help me to know that different, sad times will come to us. I will be ready to accept that and still be able to keep our ways and to be a Creek woman." The little girl lowered her head, her tears freely falling.

Her family stood watching in stunned silence. The child expressing in her simple way what they all would need to understand. Soaring Eagle broke the silence. "My Star, my brave little Star. I am so proud", her father said as he lifted her head and kissed her check.

"Thank you for helping us to understand, Morning Star," Sun Flower Woman said.

"Yes, my child, you have much wisdom for one so young," Little Flower said with tears sparkling in her own eyes.

Walking from the corner of the small cabin, Badger reached into his own pouch and removed a small green stone. "Morning Star," he said, "I would be honored if you would add this to your pouch. Hold it when you are afraid, and it will give you strength and courage."

"Thank you, Uncle Badger, "the child said, using the name he had requested that both she and Little Coyote call him. "I will. I know that fear will come to me many times."

"I know that fear will come to me too and I will not be afraid," Little Coyote said loudly. "Now, I am hungry. Can we eat?"

Everyone laughed at the little boy who had broken the serious mood that enveloped the family. "Yes, I too am hungry," Fox Slayer said, picking Little Coyote up high over his head. "Does my mother have food for her son? Then I have good news to share with my family," the young warrior said, deciding to wait to discuss the other disturbing news with his father and the other warriors at a different time.

"We have exciting news too," Little Deer said, taking the hand of her husband, Horse Stealer. "I too would like to eat now."

After the family had eaten a meal of turtle soup, baked fish and bread made from dried corn, Little Deer turned to her brother and said, "Now, tell us your good news."

"It is very good for me my sister," Fox Slayer said, smiling at his twin. Realizing that his family would not be happy about his leaving and this saddened him. "I think you should give us your news first," Fox Slayer said, having already noticed the little bump in her stomach.

Having lost two babies that were not strong enough for birth, Little Deer and Horse Stealer were excited that once again she was with child. She had gone to see Wolf Fella, the old medicine man who had healed the wounds her father had received at the Horseshoe. He still used the medicine of the grandfathers and many people had lived because of his knowledge. The eyes of the old man were weak, and his bones ached when he walked. He had taken the hand of the daughter of the man he loved as a son and together the two of them had walked the path by the little stream and found the plants and berries he would need to ensure that this baby would be strong and healthy.

Little Deer beamed as she happily announced her news. "The Great Spirit has answered my request to him. Before the time of the cold moon, I will give birth. This child will live and learn the ways of our people."

Both Little Flower and Sun Flower Woman had already guessed that Little Deer was with child but had waited until she was ready to tell them. "That is good my child," Little Flower exclaimed as she kissed her daughter.

"You should use caution," Sun Flower Woman admonished as she too hugged Little Deer.

The men nodded happily, and Soaring Eagle then turned to

his son and asked, "What is the good news that you have this day, Fox Slayer?" He suspected the news would not make him happy.

"My father and mother," Fox Slayer grinned, "you have asked many times when your son would take a wife. The time is very soon. With the next new moon, I will again travel down river to Tuckabatchee Town to make arrangements to take for my wife, Little Dove. She is the fairest maiden in all the town. She is the daughter of Chief Opothle Yahola."

Tears of both joy and sadness flowed down the face of Little Flower, Sun Flower Woman and Little Deer. They too had feared that Fox Slayer would leave Hillabee Town to seek a wife and he would need to live in the town of his wife.

"I am happy for you my son," Soaring Eagle said, feeling a lump in his throat that he tried hard to conceal. He knew he would sorely miss his son.

"Yes, Red Fox," Little Flower said, again wiping her tears away and using the name of her son's youth. "We are happy. We will greatly miss you."

"We all will go down the Tallapoosa," Sun Flower Woman chimed in. "We are invited to the ceremony are we not? And you will marry in the way of the Creek," she finished with a demanding tone.

"Yes, yes, my grandmother," Fox Slayer laughed. "All of my family will go to Tuckabatchee Town for the wedding. I know you all will love my Little Dove and we definitely will have a Creek ceremony," pausing he looked at Morning Star, the child still holding the wooden owl. "I think we have learned from my little sister on this day that while sad, difficult times may come, we are Creek people, we will continue to survive and live in the way of the Creek."

Chapter Twenty-Two
Word from Opothle Yahola

Fox Slayer made his trip to Tuckabatchee, taking with him gifts for the mother and grandmother of Little Dove, as tradition required. He also took two beautiful ponies, their brown and white coats shining in the sunlight. Chief Opothle Yahola owned a fine herd of horses and these ponies would make a nice addition.

As in times before, the first sight of Tuckabatchee was startling to the Hillabee warrior. Men, women and even the children bustled here and there as their daily activities were being attended. Today seemed to be busier than usual and Fox Slayer had encountered several warriors from other towns on the path.

Fox Slayer had just entered the outskirts of the town when he heard his name called. Turning, he saw the brother of Little Dove. "Fox Slayer, Fox Slayer," Panther called out. "It is good to see that you are back and in time. My father has called council for all the towns on the Lower Tallapoosa. You will soon be one of us and you should join in the council."

"Greetings, Panther," Fox Slayer answered, grinning at the giant warrior that loomed over his head. "When is this council?"

Looking up into the brilliant blue sky, Panther answered, "when the sun is directly overhead. You will have enough time to deliver the ponies to my father. They are intended for him, are they not?"

Fox Slayer nodded, "Yes, I would like to see your sister first as well."

"That will need to wait. She is preparing for a marriage ceremony," Panther said, laughing at the shocked look on the warrior's face.

"It is not yet time for our ceremony," Fox Slayer answered in confusion. "My family is not here."

"My brother," Panther said seriously. "The day of the marriage ceremony has been changed. I will send a fast runner to Hillabee Town immediately. Your family needs to get to Tuckabatchee in four suns. Fox Slayer, the marriage ceremony for you and my sister will take place when the sun is high the following day."

"Panther, what is the reason for this haste? My family can get here in that time, but" Fox Slayer smiled to himself, "my grandmother will not be happy."

"I have heard of grandmother Sun Flower Woman. Her strength and wisdom are known in many towns," Panther replied. "We will treat her and all of your family, especially your father well when they arrive." As he finished the single drum beat was heard. Taking the leather rope that held the ponies from Fox Slayer and giving it to a young boy with instructions to place the ponies with his father's herd, Panther said, "Fox Slayer, come, we will join the other warriors. The council will begin soon, and you will hear the reason then for the new day for the ceremony."

The two warriors hastily entered the square ground surrounded by hundreds of others from several towns along the Lower Tallapoosa. Many of the warriors were dressed in a colorful combination of Creek and the white man. Several with dark black hair falling from a wide-brim hat and the uncomfortable brogans covering their feet. Many more were clad as a Creek warrior, with turbans and moccasins donning their heads and feet and knives flashing from their belts. No matter their dress, each had something in common, a strong sense of despair and sadness filled their hearts, with only a small hope that they would not be driven from the land that had been their home since before the time of the grandfather's grandfather.

Another sharp rap of the drum silenced the crowd of Creek headmen and warriors. Their attention focusing on the man who was chieftain of the great Tuckabatchee Town. Opothle Yahola was a handsome man. His piercing eyes showed strength, but his demeanor was calm. He loved his people and they in turn had high respect and regard for him. When meeting with white leaders, he was known for dressing in striking finery, a ruffled shirt and brightly-colored scarf at his neck, covered by a brocaded hunting shirt and a plume of feathers atop his head, often being dressed better than the white men with whom he was meeting, making it clear that he was no savage. On this day, Opothle Yahola was dressed as many of the warriors, his pearl-handled knife obvious at his belt.

Stepping to the center of the square ground, Opothle Yahola nodded to the group before him and began speaking slow and clear. "Thank you, my brothers, for coming on such short notice. I am sure that, by now, each of you have heard of the deception of the Great White Father, Sharp Knife Jackson." The many before him nodded dejectedly. "Our people have suffered many, many seasons because of the greed of the white race of people. We have lost countless numbers of our brave warriors in battles we could not win. Their bones still lay in sun-drenched fields where they were slain. Many of our women have no warriors to warm their bodies in the cold of night and many of our children will never hear the voice of their father tell of the thrill of battle and of being a Creek warrior." The chieftain paused, his voice filled with emotion that he had not planned. Slowly, he continued. "The traders came first, tempting our grandfathers with their bright trinkets and axe of iron. We are your friends they said. We want to make your life better. We want nothing in return except the hide of the deer that run so freely in the forest. Then, there were no more deer. They were all gone, leaving none for food for our people. Then agents came to make us more like the white people." Opothle Yahola's voice became louder, "and the missionary and the preacher, his fiery sermons condemning the souls of the poor red man to hell." He paused again with a slight chuckle, "they did not know that we already knew about the Maker of Breath and that we thank him with the coming of each new sun." Looking out over the large crowd of Creek warriors, Opothle Yahola paused, his strength and courage becoming more evident, "we want to treat with you, the white father said. You have much land and there are some among us who would like to live in your beautiful country. Some of the grandfathers saw no harm in this and they agreed, signing a treaty and giving the white people a little of our land. This treaty led to another and another and another. The greed of the white race continued to grow. Our people were forced from their land in a place called Georgia. Our people were shamefully mistreated and moved across the River of Flowered Rocks, hoping to find peace in the land of Alabama. Soon the white people began encroaching closer and closer to our towns. After the Battle at the Horseshoe, the once great Creek Nation was reduced again, leaving only a small portion of our once majestic land for us to live. We were left alone for a few seasons, many of our people accepting the white ways and our women becoming the wives of white men. It saddens me to know that the blood of the Creek is no longer pure." Pausing once again, he smiled faintly, "still, many of our leaders and bravest warriors have the blood of the white man coursing through their veins and they have vowed never to be as the white." These words brought cheers from the large group of Creek men who just as quickly became silent again, listening to every word he chieftain spoke. "My brothers, my heart now bleeds again. The white leaders have declared that we will no longer be allowed to live on this land. This land that the Maker of Breath created for his red children. Once again, they want to treat with us. Offer us land in a different place. Give us money," shaking his head, he continued, "they do not have enough money to buy our land. I have heard that they plan to give us a small amount of land if we promise to live as they do. My brothers, I say to you this day, how can they give us land that is already ours?" More cheers and yells arose from the excited warriors. Holding up his hand, Opothle Yahola said in closing,

"I and several other chiefs will travel to Washington City, the big town of the white father. We will talk with him. We will leave in seven suns. First, I must attend the marriage ceremony of my daughter, Little Dove and the son of the Hillabee Chieftain Soaring Eagle before I talk with any white man. My brothers, I give my word of honor to you that I will stand with our people and for our people as long as I see the rays of sun of each new day. Go now, return to your homes and families. Keep this in your heart. We are Creek and we will preserver."

Chapter Twenty-Three
Little Dove

Soaring Eagle and Little Flower, along with others of their family easily made the trip to Tuckabatchee Town. Travel was much quicker now that most had horses. Sun Flower Woman had been upset about the haste in travel plans but understood when the reason was explained. The women had not been back to Tuckabatchee since the battle at the Horseshoe when they had been forced from their homes, leaving loved ones behind on the battlefield.

Memories of that past trip flooded back to them as they passed by certain places along the way, including where Little Flower had felt the living spirit of Soaring Eagle and declared that he still lived. They remembered the fear of crossing the flooded Turtle Rattle Creek, where Little Deer had slipped into the raging water and had been saved by Badger. They laughed at the defiance of a little girl as she had claimed she had not been afraid. Little Coyote listened excitedly as he heard stories of his mother's youth. Badger's heart ached as he relived the time that he had fallen in love with the beautiful Little Flower. Soaring Eagle, watching him realized that after all this time Badger still loved his wife. Soaring Eagle also realized that were it not for this man, his family would not have been taken care of and he would not have been reunited with them. Badger was a good man and Soaring Eagle knew without a doubt that he could be trusted. He had seen the brief eye contact between them at one point and knew that if he had not survived his wounds, Little Flower would now be the wife of Badger.

The group of Hillabee travelers arrived at Tuckabatchee Town just as preparations were being made for the midday meal. The women stood in awe of all the people and their activity. Little Coyote tugged on his mother's skirt and whispered, "My mother, I am afraid. There are so many people here." Morning Star reached into her pouch and tightly gripped the smooth green stone that Badger had given her for courage.

Sun Flower Woman laughed nervously and reassured the children that everything would be fine and Little Flower took the hand of her husband. The group had stood there only a short time before they were noticed. "I am Soaring Eagle. We are the family of Fox Slayer," Soaring Eagle said when asked who they were by a young warrior who smiled and told them to follow him.

As they wound their way through the town, many recognized Soaring Eagle and called out to him, making his family feel more comfortable. Arriving at the large cabin of Opothle Yahola, the family immediately saw the familiar face of Fox Slayer and by his side a beautiful maiden, her face glowing as she looked up at him.

"Father and my mother," Fox Slayer said in greeting. "And Little Deer and my grandmother and all of you. It is good that you have arrived. Please come and meet my soon to be new family." "Soaring Eagle," Opothle Yahola said, grasping the arm of the Hillabee chieftain. "My friend, I am pleased that our families will be united," looking at Little Flower and saying what he thought. "This must be your beautiful wife, Little Flower, I am honored." Turning to face the older woman, "and you are Sun Flower Woman. I have heard of your strength and courage. Welcome to Tuckabatchee."

Sun Flower Woman nodded and answered the chieftain, "Thank you. We are happy to be here."

Fox Slayer then took the hand of his soon-to-be wife and said, "My family, I would like for you to meet Little Dove, your new daughter."

The pretty young woman timidly stepped forward and smiled. Her dark black eyes sparkling in the sunlight as she looked at each of Fox Slayer's family. "Welcome," she said. "Thank you for coming. I know you must be tired from your journey. Come, I will take you to your cabins. We will have our midday meal soon," Little Dove said much too rapidly. "My mother has gone down-river to visit her sister. They are completing the dress I will wear in our marriage celebration." The young woman stopped talking and laughed, looking a Fox Slayer, "please forgive me, I have spoken too many words. I am nervous and excited." Taking the hands of Little Deer and Morning Star, she sweetly finished, "please come help me prepare our meal."

The women laughed with the animated young woman, loving her instantly. "We will be happy to help you, Little Dove," Little Flower said as she hugged her new daughter. "But first show us where we will stay." The women could be heard talking excitedly as they walked away.

The men talked briefly of the upcoming marriage ceremony which would take place in two suns. Their words quickly turned to the journey to Washington Town. "Before the sun shines over the Tallapoosa River the day after the ceremony," Opothle Yahola began. "I along with four headmen will leave to meet with Sharp Knife Jackson and his committee of men. I do not know what the result will be. I will not agree to any treaty that will remove us from our land," picking up his pipe, he sadly continued, "I fear for our people. I believe our future days will be dark." Looking at Fox Slayer he smiled, "But I do believe my daughter will be happy. Soaring Eagle, your son is a fine Creek warrior and I hope their cabin is filled with many children that will be allowed to carry on the ways of our people."

Chapter Twenty-Four
We Will Eat and Dance

Hundreds of warriors, their women and children filled the paths that led to Tuckabatchee Town. Each woman carried food; venison, turkey, fish, various early season vegetables as well as different kinds of bread made from dried corn and some even made sofkee laced with fresh honey. A few of the men secretly had bottles of firewater tucked underneath their shirts. Excitement was high, and all were in a happy mood. No one wanted to miss the marriage celebration of Chief Opothle Yahola's daughter and the warrior from Hillabee Town. Some of the warriors did wonder why Little Dove had chosen him over them, but it mattered not, for this day they all would celebrate. This event was anticipated almost as much as the Green Corn Ceremony which would take place in three moons. No one knew that ceremony would not take place during a happy time.

"My mother," Little Flower said as she braided her daughter Morning Star's jet-black hair. "Do you remember when we were preparing for the marriage celebration for me and Soaring Eagle?"

"Yes, my daughter. That is a time I will always keep close in my heart," Sun Flower Woman replied with a far-away look in her eyes, that were no longer bright with youth. "Your father and I were so proud of you and for you. I have missed him so." Tears now glistened on her cheeks. "We never knew for sure what happened to him that day at the Horseshoe. I was told by an old woman only recently that Menawa said that he saw a man that looked like your father go down. That he was shot in the back while carrying a child to safety." Sun Flower Woman covered her wrinkled face with her hands and cried not only for her husband, but for all who had died on that day so many seasons ago.

"Do not cry grandmother," Morning Star said, pulling the

green stone from her pouch. "Here, hold this and it will give you the courage when you remember the sad times." Then the little girl said softly, "And the courage to find happiness when sad times come again to us. And grandmother, they will come."

"My child," Sun Flower Woman said, wiping her tears away. "Where do you get such knowledge?" Pulling her granddaughter close she whispered, "Thank you Morning Star, you possess a special healing power that will guide you and our people through those bad times."

The sound of the drum announced that everyone should assemble at the square ground. The celebration would soon begin. Sun Flower Woman dried her eyes and smiled at her daughter and granddaughter. "Come," she said, "we do not want to be late."

The family of Fox Slayer gathered together near that of Little Dove. The mother of Little Dove smiled broadly as she excitedly talked to Little Flower, the two women had quickly become friends. "I have a special surprise for our children," she beamed and whispered, "a white preacher will perform their ceremony." Before more could be said, the drum beat silenced her. The hundreds of Creek people who had come to be a part of the celebration watched as Opothle Yahola walked to the center of the square ground and looked out over the excited crowd, thinking that soon celebrations like this might not be allowed.

"My friends and family," he said loudly. "Welcome to the wedding celebration of my daughter and the son of Soaring Eagle from Hillabee Town. As in the way of our people, Fox Slayer has presented gifts to the mother and grandmother of Little Dove," smiling he continued, "and, he has added two fine ponies to my herd of horses. He has built my daughter a large cabin and filled it with fresh deer and turkey. She has stocked their home with bread of corn and sofkee. Once these things were done, they were considered man and wife in the eyes of the Creek." He paused again, not sure how his next words would be received by some in the audience. "My people, all of you know that some of our ways are changing and we no longer live as our grandfathers." As he had expected some of the older warriors jeered in disapproval. "I agree. Even I cannot stop the change," the Tuckabatchee Chieftain said continuing. "In light of these changes, my wife and I think it best that our daughter be married by a preacher. Then, no white man can say that the marriage is not legal by white laws, no matter what happens."

A hushed silence fell over the crowd, no one wanting to argue with the chief. Some of them even thought that this could be best, as the white people did seem to have their way now. Most had never seen a white marriage ceremony and they watched with interest as a red-faced preacher, obviously nervous to be the center of attention amid hundreds of Indians, walked to the middle of the square ground. The Methodist preacher had held services for the Creek people many times before. This was different.

Opothle Yahola shook hands with the preacher in the white man way and quietly spoke to him and then turned to face the mass of Creek. "My people, now the marriage ceremony of Little Dove and Fox Slayer."

After a rapid tap of the drum, the crowd parted, and the young couple entered hand in hand. Little Deer was breathtaking. Her beautiful dark eyes shining, and her brown cheeks glowed in the sunlight. Her traditional dress was made from soft deer hide that matched her beaded white moccasins. Fox Slayer stood tall and proud. The two of them made a striking couple. With a tattered bible in his hand, the nervous preacher slowly began. "Dearly beloved, we are gathered here today to unite in holy matrimony Little Deer and Fox Slayer." He had been told to make the ceremony brief and to forego any preaching. He could, if he wished, pray for the happiness and health of the couple if he included the Giver of Breath in the prayer. The preacher did as he was told, and the ceremony was soon over, and he pronounced that Little Deer was the wife of Fox Slayer. "You may now kiss your bride," the flushed preacher quickly said, relieved that his part was over.

Not being aware of what happened at the end of a white marriage ceremony, both stood and looked at each other. A young warrior near the front of the crowd laughed and yelled out, "kiss her!"

Fox Slayer then kissed his wife and the crowd of Creek began cheering, some of the older women keened in the way of the grandmothers.

Opothle Yahola and Soaring Eagle and their families rushed to congratulate the couple. Then the Tuckabatchee Chieftain raised his hand and the people were silenced by the loud beat of the drum. "My people, we have witnessed a white marriage ceremony. Now we will celebrate in the way of our people," he paused as the large group of Creek began to cheer once again. "We will dance, and we will eat and then dance more. It is my wish that all of you enjoy yourself here at Tuckabatchee. Now, let the marriage celebration of Little Dove and Fox Slayer began. May their lives be long, and their happiness be great." As Opothle Yahola finished, many in the crowd heard the far away cry of the owl and wondered if this would be the last celebration to be held in Tuckabatchee.

Chapter Twenty-Five
We Will Not Go
Spring 1832

Two seasons had passed since the marriage ceremony and celebration of Fox Slayer and Little Dove. A tiny baby girl had been born in the cold moon season, taking her last breath in her mother's arms as the wind blew and the cry of the owl filled the night. Fox Slayer had been easily accepted and quickly became a prominent warrior in Tuckabatchee. He and Little Dove made frequent trips up the Tallapoosa to Hillabee Town to see his family. Little Dove, again with child, enjoyed being with her husband's mother and sister and Sun Flower Woman had much wisdom that she loved to share. The daughter of Little Flower had completely stolen her heart. Having seen more that twelve summers, she was no longer considered a little girl. Morning Star was now a young maiden and was known for her spiritual healing ability.

Fox Slayer and Little Dove were again in route to Hillabee. They encountered many travelers on the path, all seeming to be agitated and in a big rush. Seeing warriors from Tuckabatchee, Fox Slayer asked them the reason for the excitement. "Fox Slayer," one called out. "It is good that we have met you. We have heard from runners coming from Washington Town. My friend, the news is bad, very bad."

Nodding and already guessing, Fox Slayer asked, "The treaty?"

"Yes, the mark has been made by some of our leaders and headmen. Our chief, Opothle Yahola is now near Hillabee Town. He wishes to have words with your father before he continues to Oakfuskee and then on to Tuckabatchee. We were sent ahead to break the news to our people," the warrior answered.

"Thank you," Fox Slayer said. "We will make haste. I would like to speak with my father before Opothle Yahola arrives."

"Yes, we must go now too," the Tuckabatchee warrior said, grasping the arm of Fox Slayer. "Be alert, my friend. Our people will be in danger when word is out. The white men have been waiting for this to happen for a long time."

"Yes, they have. Use caution as well and tell the mother of my wife that I will have her daughter home before the next moon," Fox Slayer replied, climbing back onto his horse.

Fox Slayer and Little Dove quickened their pace and soon arrived in Hillabee Town. After a quick greeting to his mother and kissing his wife, he headed off to find his father. Soaring Eagle and Badger along with Horse Stealer had just returned from a short hunting trip. All three had large turkeys slung over their shoulders. Not expecting to see his son, Soaring Eagle happily said, "Fox Slayer, my son. I am happy to see you. Did you bring Little Dove with you?"

Seeing the expression on Fox Slayer's face, Soaring Eagle realized that something was wrong. "She is not sick, is she? Did she lose the baby?"

Fox Slayer smiled faintly and answered his father, "Little Dove and the baby are fine, and she is with me. My father, the removal treaty has been signed. I do not know any further details. Opothle Yahola will arrive here soon to talk with you."

Soaring Eagle, suddenly looking like an old man, sat down on the trunk of a felled tree and covered his face with his hands. Then looking up at the brilliant blue sky, he stood and slowly said, "Great Spirit, Giver of Breath, please help my people through the difficult times ahead." Turning to look at his son, Badger and Horse Stealer, he continued, "I was expecting this news. I was hoping it would not be so soon. Come, let us go prepare our family for this."

Badger placed his hand on the shoulder of his friend and spoke in a strong voice, a voice that somehow gave comfort to the Hillabee Chieftain," my brother, remember the Creek people are strong and we will preserver."

As the men returned to the village, Little Coyote, the grandson of Soaring Eagle ran to meet them and exclaimed that Chief Opothle Yahola was at their cabin visiting with his daughter. The family was engaged in a happy conversation with the father of Little Dove, who had remained quiet. The others had no idea about the grave news that he had come to relay. The returning men also said nothing, realizing this was not the time. Opothle Yahola politely asked if he and the warriors traveling with him might have food before he met with Soaring Eagle, then he would need to continue to Tuckabatchee.

After they had eaten, Opothle Yahola kissed his daughter on the cheek and told her he would see her when she returned home. Then he motioned for Soaring Eagle along with Fox Slayer, Badger and Horse Stealer to follow him. They walked a short distance from the village and sat down near the rocks where so long-ago Fox Slayer and his family had taken refuge from the white soldiers who attacked their home.
Looking at the husband of his daughter, the Tuckabatchee leader asked, "You know?"

"Yes, I met some of the runners on the path. I have also told my father," Fox Slayer answered.

"Soaring Eagle looked at Opothle Yahola, a brief look of anger crossing his face. "You signed?" he questioned.

"My friend," the chief answered sadly. "I had no choice. We have been pushed into a corner. You know that the white people of Alabama have decided that the land that belonged to us will now belong to them. They will have no mercy on us. By signing the treaty, we hope to at least save some of our land. Jackson and the white leaders in Washington City said they will protect us from the onslaught of the greedy whites. The leaders of Alabama will not." The Chief paused, rubbing his eyes, he was very tired, "Some of our Creek people have already gone to Indian Territory, many more say they will go. Not only will be stripped of our land and homes, but no longer will be allowed our laws and ceremonies. We will be forced to live as the whites if we stay."

Just A Cotton Field

"The land they say that will still belong to us," Soaring Eagle said quietly, "no longer angry with the Tuckabatchee leader, "I have heard about this. Can you tell me how this will come to be?"

"We, the chiefs and headmen of the towns will be issued large tracks or allotments in what the white men call acres of land. Others will receive smaller amounts," Oplothle Yahola answered.

"Do they not realize that the land is already ours? How can they give us our own land?" the Hillabee leader agitatedly asked.

"Did you not hear me, my friend," the Tuckabatchee Chief asked, trying not to become exasperated. "The white people plan to take from us what is ours. They think they have every right to do so."

"I understand completely," Soaring Eagle said, trying to keep his composure. "They have no right and my people do not understand allotment. You know all Creek people own the land. It does not belong to any one man. And," he continued, "this land across the big river, we do not know if even corn will grow there, and the streams may have no fish and the forest no deer. My people will not go. We will stay on our land until they drive us away like cattle," Soaring Eagle paused, looking intently at Opothle Yahola. "My chief promise me you will do what you can to save the homes of our people."

The strong words of his friend had excited and given hope to Opothle Yahola. He too looked deeply into the eyes of the other man, understanding the deep love he had for his people. "Soaring Eagle, my brother, the words you say are true. There are many of the Tuckabatchee people who will not leave until they are forced, and I am one of them. I promise you, and our people that I will fight, not with a bow and arrow or musket of old, but with the words of truth. This land does belong to the Creek people."

Chapter Twenty-Six
Surveyors on Creek Land

Morning Star, now well into her fourteenth season, had continued to learn the ways of her grandmothers and considered it her responsibility to help those who were low in spirit or feared for the future. She had also learned which plants to use to cure sickness. She and son of her sister, Little Coyote continued to spend much time together and now his little sister, Blue Bird, begged to tag along on excursions into the forest to search for leaves and berries that were needed to help the sick both spiritually and physically.

They had ventured farther up the path by Cedar Creek today than she intended. Morning Star had been warned that it was too dangerous to go so far from Hillabee Town, but she needed just a little more of the bear grass that she used for so many remedies. Little Coyote saw them first. "Star, look," he said quietly as he pointed across the creek. Only a short distance away, four white men, two of them holding strange metal sticks were walking toward them.

Morning Star pulled the little girl closer to her as she and Little Coyote watched the men come nearer. Not realizing the danger, the child innocently and loudly asked, "Star, who are they?" Morning Star quickly placed her hand over Blue Bird's mouth.

The men had heard the child and looked in the direction of Morning Star and the children. They had been seen and there was no place to go. "You there, stop," one of the men, dressed as a white preacher called out, his black string tie flapping in the breeze.

Having no choice, Morning Star took the small hand of Blue Bird and whispered to Little Coyote to remain silent. She waited as the men crossed the small creek on stones that protruded from the water. "Who are you and why are you here," one of the other men asked, speaking with an accent that was not familiar to Morning Star.

Not clearly understanding him, she said nothing, reaching her free hand into her pouch, tightly gripping the smooth green stone.

"I said who are you?" the man repeated harshly.

"Jack, you know she's just an injun and these people don't know how to talk English, a third man added, spitting tobacco juice from his mouth, much of which splattered on his filthy shirt.

"And a right pretty little one," the fourth man proclaimed." He too was unclean, his long flaxen hair escaping from a faded red ribbon.

Taking a deep breath, Morning Star answered. "I am Morning Star. My father is Soaring Eagle, Chief of the Hillabee. We are searching for bear grass."

"Well, this little lassie is also smart," the man with long hair said, his eyes raking over Morning Star as he stepped closer to her. "I bet you ah sweet thing too," he said, reaching out to touch her hair.

"Leave her be Edgar, we are here to survey their land not to take their women or their little girls," the string-tie man said. He had not trusted or cared for these ruffians that had been hired to guide he and George over Indian land.

In a flash Little Coyote had jumped from Morning Star's side and began kicking the man angrily on his knee. Just as quickly, his buddy pulled the child away from the surprised man. "Yeh, little injun brat, get away from him." The filthy man said as he pushed the child down. The two surveyors stood in shocked silence watching the scene before them. They feared that if they tried to intervene, they might also be in danger. These men had no honor and would think nothing of killing them and these children.

Morning Star helped Little Coyote to his feet, seeing blood run down his arm. She quietly whispered for him to take his sister and slowly back away and then run for safety. He shook his head indicating that he would not leave her. "Go." She mouthed as she turned to face their assailants, placing her hand back into her pouch.

"What cha got in that pouch, pretty little thing," Edgar said as he moved toward her again.

Morning Star bravely looked at the man, no longer afraid. As she pulled the owl and the eyeless doll from her pouch, the chilling cry of a real owl filled the air. Both men jumped. "An owl in the middle of the day? What does this mean?" Then looking at what the girl had in her hand they began to step away from her. "A doll with no eyes and a wooden owl with eyes that stare right at you. What are ya, a witch or sompin?" Edgar asked, his voice cracking.

All four men jumped at the deep sound of a man's voice. "No, she is not a witch. A medicine woman and beloved woman, but not a witch," Badger said, taking Morning Star's hand and pulling her closer to him. He had been alarmed when the children had not returned and had met Little Coyote and Blue Bird on the path. He had witnessed the actions of both the men and Morning Star.

"Uncle Badger," she said softly, suddenly feeling weak. She did not know how long she could have kept the filthy white man away from her and the other two white men seemed to be of no help.

Badger turned to them, his eyes cold and his voice threatening, "You would stand by and let these vermin harm this young woman? Who are you and what is your purpose here," he asked angrily.

"We are surveyors hired by the United States Government to mark off this land," Jack answered not comfortable with this Indian man in front of him.

"The land on this side of the creek belongs to the Hillabee and you have no business here. I strongly advise you to get back on the other side before I signal for the Hillabee warriors to come and assist me. Go."

Just A Cotton Field *117*

Badger and Morning Star watched the four intruders cross back over White Oak Creek, the one called Edgar remarked, "I still think that girl's ah witch." The cry of the owl became softer and Badger looked at Morning Star, smiling, "Come, let us go home."

Chapter Twenty-Seven
This Is Our Home

Life in Hillabee Town continued in a slow, easy pace, much as it had in the past. The women and children planted corn and beans in small gardens near their cabins. The men continued to hunt, but only for small game within the boundaries of the town. Several babies had been born in the last season and some of the old ones had walked the path of the Great Spirit.

Soaring Eagle and his headmen took pride in maintaining stability in the Hillabee Town when much of the Creek Nation was in a state of great despair. Almost immediately after the Washington Treaty was ratified, the whites began crowding into the nation in alarming numbers. Andrew Jackson and his federal government tried in vain to control the land-hungry whites, telling them to wait at least until the surveyors could do their job and the Creek land could be divided into allotments. The State of Alabama did little to quail the tide of intruders.

Smoke from their pipes drifted above the heads of the men as they sat around a dying fire. The sun had long since set and the sound of the night, the tree frogs, the whippoorwill and the distant coyotes began their crescendo all in unison.

"The whippoorwill and brother coyote have sad calls this night," Soaring Eagle said to no one in particular. A strong feeling of melancholy had enveloped him that he could not seem to escape.

"The sounds of nature in our country are sad, but also beautiful," Badger added, stirring the fire. He too felt a strong, unexplainable sadness. When the mournful call of the owl began he continued, "The owl, oh the owl. We all know what sadness he brings this time."

"Remember what Mourning Star told us?" Soaring Eagle spoke softly. "The owl does not bring the sad, difficult times, but is warning us so that we may prepare for what the future days will bring."

Nodding his head, Badger agreed. "Yes, and I think we should begin our preparations. I met other Creek on the Oakfuskee path today. I was told that a new surge of whites has entered the nation. They boldly come up to the cabins of our people and order them to leave, that the cabin no longer belongs to them."

Fox Slayer added in agreement. "I too have heard from Opothle Yahola that white families are encroaching nearer and nearer to Tuckabatchee. Few of our people understand this allotment plan and how it works," he laughed ruefully, "and the white leaders knew they would not. Thank you, my father for seeing through this ruse of the evil whites."

"Yes, we all are safe here," Soaring Eagle paused, "for now, anyway. We must prevent any of our people from falling into the trap and selling any of their land to the white tricksters. It would only take one Hillabee to sell and then we would become like many other towns."

"I was also told," Badger began, "that some of the Creek men are tempted by the white firewater and sell their land, having no idea what they are doing, and that many, many of our people are hungry with no homes and nowhere to go."

Horse Stealer had been silent, listening to his wife's family talk. "My brothers," he began, "I have heard that even in my old town on the Chattahoochee, people are hungry and destitute. Many of them have given up and have or plan to make the move to Indian Territory. Do you think that…"

"No," Soaring Eagle said adamantly. "We will stay until we are forced to leave. This is the land the Giver of Breath made for us. This is our home."

Chapter Twenty-Eight
We Are Hungry

Conditions continued to deteriorate all over the Creek Nation. Many more of the Creek people were hungry, wandering from settlement to settlement, begging for food and shelter. Some even went so far as to go to the homes of white families, employing them to give food, if only for the children. Occasionally, a kind woman would give them bread, but more often, a musket was pointed at them and they were told to leave.

Land speculators were rampart, fraudulently taking land from the Creeks, almost before the allotments were issued. The United States Government had promised equal land in Indian Territory and payment would be made for the sale of allotted land. If any money was issued, greedy white men were standing by to take it from the Creeks. "This injun owes me money, or this one stole my horse." After the transaction, the Creek had nothing, no land, no money or any form of sustenance. The pressure was great and first one small group and then another gave in and put their mark on papers indicating that they would go. This applied to Hillabee Town as well.

Morning Star was no longer a child, having seen sixteen cold seasons. Respect for her ability to heal both physically and spiritually had continued to grow. She was very beautiful and kind-hearted and under normal circumstances, many young warriors would have watched her dance, but there were no dances or any celebrations. The sad cloud that had been cast over the entire Creek Nation now covered Hillabee. The Hillabee people did fair slightly better. They still had food and were always willing to share.

In search of plants that provided her medicine, Morning Star was walking in the woods and found herself near the remains of the Grierson Farm. As she came in sight of the cabin of Sinnugee, she saw a wagon filled with colorful blankets and neatly woven baskets and two brightly painted chest placed side by side with pots and cooking utensils dangling from the side. Sinnugee came from her cabin, her eyes red and swollen. "Grandmother Sinnugee," Morning Star said hesitantly. "Are you leaving?"

"Yes, Morning Star. I am so glad that you came today. I wanted to see you one final time. My son and daughter said that we cannot stay any longer. We will go to Indian Territory," the woman said sadly, with decades of time and sorrow showing on her wrinkled face.

"I am sorry Sinnugee," Morning Star answered with tears in her own eyes. "I will miss you. You have helped me much in learning the ways of a medicine woman."

"I have only showed you the way, Morning Star. The gift was already in you." Reaching into the pocket of her apron, Sinnugee pulled out a small item securely wrapped in weathered deerskin. "When you are alone, open this. It will continue to show you the way."

"Mother, come," the son of Sinnugee called out. "It is time for us to go."

Sinnugee pulled Morning Star close and held her tight. "Oh, Little Star. This is so hard. I will never see you or my home again. May the Great Spirit look over you, my child." The forlorn old woman released the girl and climbed onto the wagon. She looked straight ahead, never looking back. Morning Star, with tears streaming down her face, watched her leave. Her heart aching when she heard the sorrowful keening of her friend. Reaching inside her pouch, she pulled out the small package and slowly unwrapped the deerskin. Gasping as she looked at the clear-faceted stone in her hand, she said out loud, "Oh Sinnugee, now I understand. The crystal will show me the way and I will help our people."

Morning Star sadly and slowly walked back to Hillabee, so deep in her thoughts she completely walked past a large clump of berries that she needed. Realizing this, she turned to go back. As she stooped to pick the berries she saw a family of forlorn Creek people on the path. Their clothing torn and tattered, the woman carrying a small child, had no moccasins on her feet. Seeing the young woman, the man cautiously asked, "Please, do you have food? We have walked many miles in many days. We cannot go much farther."

"Yes, my family has food," Morning Star answered. "Come, follow me."

Morning Star led the family back to Hillabee Town and went directly to the cabin of Soaring Eagle and Little Flower. "My mother, these people are hungry. Do we have food for them?"

"Yes, I have big pot of sofkee on the fire. Get the bowls for me," Little Flower answered as she turned to look at the family before her. She was instantly filled with pity and then recognition. She had seen this woman before. "I am Little Flower, wife of Soaring Eagle."

The woman gasped, "Is this Hillabee Town? This is the town of my birth. Do you remember me? I was made a slave when we were taken to Coweta after the Horseshoe," the woman said rapidly.

"Yes, I do remember you," Little Flower said. "Please eat and then we will talk. Morning Star, your father is with Badger and Horse Stealer. Please go to the cabin of your sister and ask him to come."

The man nodded his head in appreciation as he took the bowl of steaming sofkee. "Yes, I have words to say to Soaring Eagle that he should hear."

The starving family had finished eating when Morning Star returned with her father. Badger and Horse Stealer had come as well. Little Deer and Morning Star with the woman and her two children had gone to the cabin of Sun Flower Woman, hoping to secure a pair of moccasins and a dress for the woman.

The men sat outside the cabin, ready to hear what words the visitor had to say. "Soaring Eagle," he began. "As you know, we are from Coweta," the man paused, "like many others, I was foolish and lost my allotment of land. We had to leave. We have no where to go. We have wandered from village to village for many moons. There are many Creek people in the same situation as we are, but you already know that," he paused again. "There are some of our people on the Alabama side of the Chattahoochee who think we should fight to keep our land. Already Creek warriors are marauding and killing white settlers, even women and children."

"People of Coweta are involved in this?" Badger asked.

"Yes, some are. Most are Hitchitti and Euchee and a few from Talisi and Loachapoka. I did not want to be a part of this," the tired Creek man said.

"This is not good. The Creek people could not win the first time and they certainly cannot win now," Soaring Eagle said sadly. "This will only make the situation worse. We should go immediately to Oakfuskee to talk with Menawa."

Chapter Twenty-Nine
We Are Too Old to Fight

The following morning Soaring Eagle, Badger and Horse Stealer left Hillabee for Oakfuskee. The Hillabee leader had been alarmed by the news received from the Creek man from Coweta. He understood that some of the warriors near the eastern border of the nation still had the spirit of the Red Stick Warriors of the past. He too felt that strong spirit coursing through him, but his people had to be sensible. They were so few now as the bones of most of the Red Stick Warriors lay on battlefields, scattered across the Creek Nation. Menawa would know best how to handle this uprising. The old chief had fought with all his strength and soul during the Creek War and still suffered from injuries he had received at the Horseshoe. Soaring Eagle knew the wisdom of his old friend would prevail.

The Hillabee warriors had traversed the path to Oakfuskee often and this trip took only a short time arriving before the sun was directly overhead. Oakfuskee was a much larger town than Hillabee and even more so now as the mass of destitute Creek people flocked into the town. The men went directly to the cabin of Menawa. He was sitting outside talking quietly with some of his headmen, his pipe, as always in his hand. Looking up, he noticed his visitors immediately.

"Ah, Soaring Eagle, my old friend," the old chief said in greeting. "I have been expecting you. You have heard about the foolishness of some of our people," Menawa said standing.

"Yes, Menawa, why would they do this? Do they not realize what this will mean?" Soaring Eagle asked as the two friends clasped arms.

"Sit down and join us. Our women will bring our midday meal soon," the chief said, nodding at Badger and Horse Stealer. "We are now discussing these actions. Soaring Eagle, these warriors, and that is what they consider themselves, are desperate. This is their last effort to save our country," shaking his head, Menawa smiled faintly and continued, "this will not work. The old and young fools will only get themselves killed, but the white people are scared as a rabbit scampering through the forest. They are leaving their farms and running to the big town called Columbus across the Chattahoochee," he laughed out loud. "So, the Hitchiti and Eunchee are helping themselves to the livestock and anything else they want. Again, I say this is foolish, but were I a young man, I too would paint my face red."

Soaring Eagle smiled, shaking his head in agreement. "What will you do my chief? We are no longer young and are too wise to be a part of these actions."

"Opothle Yahola and I will travel to the eastern border of what is left of our nation to talk with the warriors. We will tell them it is too late for us. It will soon be time for us to leave the land of our grandfathers. It is time for us to go," the old man said as unashamed tears rolled down his wrinkled face.

Chapter Thirty
Her Bones Will Lie Here

Only a few suns had passed when Soaring Eagle received word from Menawa that more than words would be needed to quail the uprising. In an ironical twist of events, government officials had requested help from the friendly Creeks to calm the warriors that continued to burn the farms of the white settlers. Several whites had been killed and these actions had to be stopped. Menawa asked for aid from the Hillabee to assist the Oakfuskee and the Tuckabatchee with this request.

Soaring Eagle was not surprised when both Badger and Horse Stealer along with many other Hillabee warriors said they would go immediately to join with warriors from Tuckabatchee. He guessed and was correct that his son too would offer his service.

"My brothers," Soaring Eagle said as his friend and husband of his oldest daughter were preparing to leave. "I pray to the Great Spirit for your safe return. I urge you to use caution and do not place yourself in any unnecessary danger. I too would go, but I feel that I can better serve our people by staying here."

"Take care of our family, my brother," Badger stated, both men realizing that he considered them his family too. "Our people also will need your guidance. I feel that our time here in our home is short," he sadly said as he hugged Soaring Eagle forgoing the normal arm clasp of warriors. "Come, Horse Stealer, let us gather the others who will go with us."

Little Deer held tightly to her husband. She whispered softly that she loved him and then cried loudly, "Horse Stealer, my husband, please come back to me and our children," wiping a tear from her eye, she smiled. "I mean that."

Horse Stealer kissed his wife and picked up his daughter, swinging her high in the air, "Blue Bird, be good and do as your mother ask," he then turned to his son, who was quickly becoming a young warrior. "Little Coyote take care of your mother and sister."

"My father," Little Coyote answered, "I will. Be safe."

Both men then turned to Little Flower and Sun Flower Woman. Horse Stealer hugged the mother and grandmother of his wife. Badger kissed Little Flower quickly on the cheek, not allowing himself to think of the love he still felt for her. She smiled at him, knowing his thoughts. "Take care, Badger."

Sun Flower Woman followed Badger and Horse Stealer when they walked away from the cabin. She called out to Badger, asking him to stop. "Badger, I have words I need to say before you go."

"Yes, Sun Flower Woman, what is it you wish to tell me?" Badger asked with respect for the old woman he had known for so long.

"My son," she began, the sunlight shining brightly on her face showed only faintly the beautiful spirited woman she once had been. "Badger, I need to thank you for the care and compassion you have shown me and my family, from the time of the Horse Shoe and during the period when we stayed with your family on the River of Flowered Rocks. Your heart is filled with kindness and I know we would never have survived were it not for you." She paused, smiling, "I also know of your love for my daughter. Now, I must tell you farewell," she finished, her voice breaking.

"Sun Flower Woman, I will return," Badger answered, surprised.

"You will, but I feel in my heart that I will never see you again." The old woman slowly turned away, keening softly.

Badger was disturbed by the words of Sun Flower Woman and had walked only a short distance when he again heard his name. Morning Star had been, as she often was, searching for plants and berries.

"Badger, Uncle Badger," she called out. "Do not leave yet. I must tell you to use care. I fear there will be danger in this journey." She stood on the tip of her toes and kissed the tall warrior's cheek.

"I will be very cautious, Morning Star. Has your grandmother been acting any different? Do you think she is sick or, or …" Badger stopped, not knowing how to finish."

"Yes, Uncle Badger, grandmother Sun Flower Woman has lost the strong spirit that has always given her strength. I have talked with her," Morning Star softly continued. "She will not leave the home of her grandmothers. He bones will lie here, not in a strange land, in a faraway place."

Chapter Thirty-One
Red Streaked Stone

The grip of the white man continued to tighten. Their patience with the Creek had grown thin. These people would either move to Indian Territory on their own or be forced by whatever method was necessary. The choice was theirs, but the red people would leave this land. It no longer belonged to them. Cotton needed to be planted in this rich fertile soil.

The Hillabee people as with all the Creek and Cherokee, now realized that time was running out for them. Some had already established themselves in their new homes. Those who had left earlier had fared better than those who had waited to go. The government now hired removal agents to lead the way. Many of the agents were unscrupulous white men looking for any way to take everything from the poor unfortunate Indian. Some would be taken north, and the entire trip would be overland, while others would be taken to the river towns where they boarded small boats for the remainder of the way. Still others went south to Mobile and were packed onto big boats that belched steam and made loud frightening sounds.

The government officials and the removal agents decided the quickest and most efficient method to move these people would be in large groups. First, they needed to be rounded up and taken to holding stockades until the time came to leave for Indian Territory.

Runners had been dispatched to Hillabee Town from Opothle Yahola, telling Soaring Eagle not to agree to leave. The Tuckabatchee Chieftain was still negotiating with government officials and all the warriors, including Menawa and the family of Soaring Eagle had not yet returned from the eastern part of the nation. Many of the Red Stick warriors, had been brought in, while others still hid deep in the swamps between the Chattahoochee and the Tallapoosa. The Second Creek War, as it was called, was all but over and again victory was claimed by the white man. The warriors had tried in vain to save their homeland, but they too knew it was time to go, but they did not realize what still lay ahead for their people.

****

The mockingbird sang her sweet tune and the rays of the morning sun danced on the treetops of the now much smaller Hillabee village. Fewer fires had been started to prepare the morning meal. Most of the people were gone, the removal agents lining them up to march them off to different holding stockades to wait and wait. Soaring Eagle had informed the threatening men that his family would not go. That some of them had gone with Menawa to round up the hostiles. He would wait until their return and then join other family members in Tuckabatchee. They would leave with Opothle Yahola. The brave warrior who had survived the Horseshoe and refused to be intimidated by these white men who smelled of firewater and used coarse, vile words. One of them smiled evilly and spit the brown juice of tobacco on the ground as he walked away. He was heard to say, "We will be back."

From inside the cabin, Little Flower, Sun Flower Woman and the children had watched as the men walked away. "My mother, I am so afraid," she whispered, pulling her family near her.

Sun Flower Woman had a far away look in her eyes and softly answered her daughter, "You must be brave. Remember, I have always taught you that. My Little Flower, I love you and Soaring Eagle and all of my family," the old woman continued, "you will go to the new land and I will remain here."

"Mother, what do you mean, that you will stay here," Little Flower admonished.

"My daughter, I am old, and my bones hurt. I cannot make this journey," Sun Flower Woman said, wiping tears from her daughter's face. "And if I could, I would not go. I will forever be in the land of our grandmothers and your father, oh your father. I remember, so well his farewell kiss when he left us at the Horseshoe." Sun Flower Woman paused, touching her own face. "Come, let us prepare our morning meal. I am hungry. We will talk no more of this. I have said my words."

Little Flower stared at her mother and begin to speak when Morning Star placed her hand on her mother's arm and shook her head. "Yes, my mother, we are hungry, and we should eat. Let us prepare a special meal this day." Morning Star felt a sense of dread as she pulled the crystal from her pouch and watched as red streaked the clear stone.

Chapter Thirty-Two
Be Strong

The family of Soaring Eagle sat in silence as they finished their morning meal. The chatter of the cheerful mockingbird became silent and was replaced by the mournful cry of the owl. Soaring Eagle looked at his family, seeing fear in their eyes. The owl became silent and suddenly the door was kicked open. Little Deer screamed, and Soaring Eagle reached for his musket. The same foul-mouthed, filthy white man they had seen earlier, followed by two other men who looked equally disgusting entered the cabin.

"What do you mean coming into my cabin?" Soaring Eagle yelled, "Get out!"

"No, don't think I will, injun," the man answered in a jeering tone. "Think it'll be you and your pretty little family that'll be getting out. And I'll jest take your gun."

As Soaring Eagle stepped toward the man, he was jumped from behind by the other men, one of them grabbing the old musket. Little Deer screamed again and pulled Blue Bird closer to her.

"Shut up. You pretty little woman," the man said, looking around the cabin to see if he saw anything of value that he wanted. From out of the dark corner where he had been standing, Little Coyote jumped onto the back of one of the men who held Soaring Eagle down. "Get off of me you little heathen," the surprised intruder yelled, pushing Coyote down on the dirt floor.

Morning Star quickly grabbed an iron pan and attempted to hit the man over the head. He looked up just in time to receive only a glancing blow. She too was pushed to the floor. Realizing that these evil men would think nothing of killing all his family, Soaring Eagle loudly proclaimed, "Let me up and tell me what it is that you want of us."

One of the men roughly pulled the Hillabee Chieftain up and then pushed him toward his family who had watched in horror at what had transpired. Morning Star and Coyote stood up, both rubbing their arms and took their place beside Little Flower and Little Deer.

"I done told you," the leader of the three replied. "You no longer can stay here. You will go jest like the rest of you thieving red-skinned people. This here is white folks land now."

"And I told you," Soaring Eagle stated, his voice rising, "Opothle Yahola is my friend and my family…"

"I don't care what ya said. My orders is to move you out of here and by dang it, I'm gonna do that." The man who identified himself as Pete continued, "I guess you are in luck. You said you wanted to go down river and that's where we're going. We got us bout twenty-five of you Hillabee people and we will pick us up more as we go."

Soaring Eagle starred at the man called Pete, his dark eyes flashing in anger. "When do we go?"

"Now, you injun fool. Take only what you can carry." Looking around the sparse cabin, he continued, "you shore don't have much do you? Not like them uppity Cherokee, but I think I can use that pretty basket over there. My little woman I got at home will really like that."

"We need time to get our blankets and," Little Flower began.

"I said weze going now," Pete yelled as he picked up the basket.

"My mother and daughter need to go to their cabin to get their…"

"I said be quiet woman. If their cabin is in the direction weze going, they can git blankets, if not…" he shrugged his shoulders. "Go, start walking now."

Soaring Eagle dejectedly led his family out of their home. He had not felt such desolation since the time of the Horseshoe. "Oh, Great Spirit," he thought, "please be with us."

Sun Flower Woman had not spoken. She slowly walked to her cabin. Not coming out immediately, Pete yelled, "Old woman, get out here now!"

Sun Flower Woman slowly came out the door, a leather string filled with red beads were tightly clasped in her hand. The tired old woman who had been the spirit of the Red stick women looked at her daughter and grandchildren and smiled, "Be strong and keep the ways of our people." She turned and walked away.

"Old woman, you go'in the wrong way," Pete yelled out. "Get back here. Don't make me put a rope on ya."

Sun Flower Woman slowly sank to the ground. "Mother, my mother," Little Flower screamed as she ran to the woman. Soaring Eagle quickly joined his wife, fearing what had just happened. He slowly turned the woman over. The face of the mother of his wife no longer looked old and sad, but at peace. He took Little Flower into his arms and held her close.

Little Flower, with tears streaming down her face, looked at her mother and then noticed the string of red beads that had fallen from her hand. "My father," she said softly. "These beads belonged to my father." She slowly picked the string up and placed them around Sun Flower Woman's neck. Little Flower looked at her husband and softly asked, "Did you hear?"

"Yes," Soaring Eagle answered with tears in his eyes. "I heard her say, be strong. She is on the path to the Great Spirit now. Her bones will remain here with your father and the grandmothers, just as she has said."

Chapter Thirty-Three
Snap of a Whip

Terrified by what had just happened, the removal agents allowed the family of Sun Flower Woman a few minutes alone with their love one. They then were told to quickly bury the woman in whatever fashion was necessary. No time would be permitted for any ceremony. They had orders to move these people down river and they were already behind schedule.

Tearfully, Little Flower and her family did as they were told. Placing an old worn blanket on the stones that covered the grave of her mother, Little Flower wondered where she would find the strength to carry on. "My mother," Morning Star whispered softly, tears streaming down her own face. "Remember, we must be strong. The white men are tired of waiting and we must move on." The beautiful young woman slowly reached into her pouch and first removed the doll with no eyes, the crystal given to her by Sinnugee and then the shinny green stone that Badger said would help her to find the way and give her courage. She gripped the stone tightly.

Soaring Eagle looked at the men who had watched the family closely. "I am chief of the few who remain at Hillabee Town. I have words to say to my people. You are forcing us from our homes that we will never see again. I demand that you give us a short time to prepare for this journey."

Pete saw the look of ice in the eyes of Soaring Eagle. Something about these people had unnerved him and he realized that they could overpower him and the others if they tried. Looking at the sun, Pete answered roughly, "When you see the sun reach the top of that big tree over yonder, we will go. Say your words to your people now."

Soaring Eagle nodded and gathered his family and the twenty or so other people around him. This was all that remained. The rest had already gone. Where, he wasn't sure. "My people," the chieftain began, his voice breaking. "This is the day we knew would come. We have no choice and no more time. I do not know what lies ahead for us. I do know that we are Hillabee. We are part of the great Creek Nation and we will survive. Look one final time at our home and the land of our grandfathers." Pausing, Soaring Eagle waved his arms, encompassing the area around them. "Let us go now and take the spirit of the ancient ones with us."

Taking the hand of Little Flower, with Little Deer, Coyote and Blue Bird behind them, Soaring Eagle led the remainder of the Hillabee down the path. He knew that his youngest daughter had unfinished matters to take care of and that she would catch up. Morning Star was communing not only with the recently departed spirit of her grandmother, but of all the grandmothers before her. She would need their guidance to help her people.

The Hillabee walked in silence, many in tears, some of the women began keening. Feeling a strange sense of comfort overwhelm her, Little Flower began to sing an old song of the grandmothers, one that Sun Flower Woman had sung many seasons ago when the Hillabee women were taken to the River of Flowered Rocks.

Soaring Eagle, his family and the small group of Hillabee followed the man called Pete along a path that he himself knew better than the guide. They were on foot now, their horses had long-since been taken by the white man who had claimed them as their own. Their load was light, being told to bring only what they could carry. The family of Soaring Eagle had wisely bundled a few belongings inside their blankets, most of the others had not. The sun was well past its midpoint in the sky and they still walked, not even stopping for water. Some of the group were old and many were children. They could not keep up with the pace of Pete, riding comfortably on a fine stallion, one taken from an up-river village. The other two white men brought up the rear, they too were on Indian ponies. Time after time the sharp snap from a whip was heard as the Hillabee group began to walk slower.

Hearing the whip snap again, Soaring Eagle stopped and ordered his family to wait. "I am going back to put a stop to this. My people will not be herded like cattle." Pete had gotten well ahead of the group and did not notice that they had stopped. "Coyote, stay here and tell him," pointing to Pete, "that your grandfather had to check on the children and old women. Do not let him harm your mother or grandmother. I will not be gone long."

Walking back to the end of the line, Soaring Eagle immediately saw that his people were frightened. They were trying to stay ahead of the men and away from the whip. Just as one of them raised his arm again to crack his whip, Soaring Eagle called out, "Stop! Put that whip away. Do not harm any of my people."

"We will use the whip when we get ready and will take none of your smart injun talk," one of them said, the whip snapping again in the air, the Hillabee scrambling to get far enough away to avoid the smart sting.

Hot rage filled Soaring Eagle and he placed his hand on the knife in his legging, pausing he stopped. These men did not know about his knife. All weapons were supposed to have been surrendered before they left Hillabee Town. He had managed to hide his and he knew several other warriors still had theirs as well. There might be a greater need later for a knife. Soaring Eagle had not realized that his daughter had followed him until she touched his arm.

"My father, I will help you get our people moving again," she boldly said, looking at the white men, before turning to look at her father entreating him to calm down. She knew they would enjoy using the whip on him. "I do not think these men will use their whip again. I know we should continue to move." She turned back to the Hillabee people who watched in amazement, the actions of the brave young woman.

"My daughter is right, and we should move on. Come, my people, let us go," Soaring Eagle ordered in complete control. He saw his daughter turn back to the dumb-founded men. She pulled the doll with no eyes and the crystal again from her pouch. The men watched as she gazed intently at both before looking up at them.

"My people will survive," she proclaimed. "And you will not harm them." Morning Star quickly turned away and joined her father and her people. The mournful cry of the owl again filled the silence.

"What did she just do?" One of the men asked. "Did she call up that owl?"

"I don't know," the other said. "She has some kind of power and I ain't messing with her or her father or any of them injun people."

"Yeah, I'll be glad to turn them over to somebody else at the holding pin," the jittery man said, putting away the whip.

Chapter Thirty-Four
The Holding Pen

The Hillabee People continued their journey, thinking they were going to Tuckabatchee Town. They had spent their first night at Oakfuskee where food was provided by the unsuspecting Oakfuskee people. The next morning, many of them were told just as the Hillabee, that time was up, and they must go. Little Flower and her daughter attempted to comfort the distraught women as they joined them on the trail, their keening loud and sad. One aging woman, who had spent many seasons at Oakfuskee, cut her hair and scratched her arms as the Creek women had done in times of mourning in the past.

The group had now increased to more than sixty and other removal agents, as they called themselves, had arrived from out of the woods. These ruffians were coarse, crude men who cared little about the safety or wellbeing of the Creek people. Their job was to move these injuns out of their homes and most importantly to pick up the bag of coins they would be paid. These men were not the soldiers the government had promised would take the Creek to their new home.

Soaring Eagle continued his role as leader of the group. He had talked to the Oakfuskee men, warning them of the danger of resisting. "Do as you are told," he had said. "These men will slaughter all of us if provoked."

Pete also had talked with the new group of agent men, telling them to beware of the Hillabee leader and especially his pretty daughter. "I think she may be a witch. She calls up owls in the middle of the day and carries a doll with no eyes."

The Hillabee and Oakfuskee, tired and weary, trudged on. The ruthless men pushed them to keep walking and the food that was provided was not fit for them to eat. Turtle Rattler Creek had been easily crossed on a hewed wooden bridge built by recent white settlers to the area now called Realtown. A new

Just A Cotton Field

settlement that had been named after the O'Real brothers who operated a trading post.

Soaring Eagle stopped his people. Turning to look at them, Pete loudly called out, "Why have you stopped? I did not tell you to stop."

"My people need to rest, if only for a short time. They are thirsty and hungry. Is there no more food?" Soaring Eagle employed. "We are only one sun from Tuckabatchee, if we are allowed to rest."

"Tuckabatchee," Pete laughed. "You ain't going there."

Confused, Soaring Eagle frowned. "Where are you taking us then?"

"To a place called Pole Cat Springs, on the other side of the big river, down from Tuckabatchee.

"They got a big ole pen, that'll hold a lot," making fun of the Hillabee leader he continued, "of your people. I reckon the pen will be full and pretty soon y'all will be on your way." Laughing again, "To some where's else. That'll leave more land for my people. Shore is some mighty fine land down there for growing cotton." Looking at the forlorn people behind Soaring Eagle, he did feel just a little sorry for them. "Yeah, let them rest for a while, and even eat, if they can find some berries or somp'un. I have no more food to give 'em.

Soaring Eagle relayed the message to the Hillabee and Oakfuskee. Some of the older ones sank to the ground for much needed rest, while others scavenged along the path for any edible vegetation or berries. He saw no reason to tell the group that they were not going to Tuckabatchee. He would need to tell his family.

"Come, my family. Let us rest under that big oak tree. I have information you should know."

Smiling, Morning Star pulled a handful of dried corn from her pouch and divided it with her family. "I knew we would need this," she said. "My father, what is the news we need to hear? I know it will not be good."

"You are correct, my daughter," Soaring Eagle sadly answered. "We are not being taken to Tuckabatchee Town. We are going to Pole Cat Springs to a big holding pen, to be held like we are cattle." Soaring Eagle covered his weary face with his huge brown hands, "My family, I can do nothing to prevent this. I cannot save you or our people."

Little Flower and the children sat in silence. Morning Star pulled the crystal from her pouch, looking intently to the now cloudy stone. "My father," she said, "Opothle Yahola will help us."

Suddenly Blue Bird looked up at Little Deer. "My mother, where is my father? Is he coming back and, and," the little girl began to cry, "Uncle Fox Slayer and Uncle Badger, when can we see them?"

Little Deer looked at her father with questioning eyes, eyes which overflowed with tears she had tried to hold back, but no longer could. "Father, have you heard any news about them? Where are they?" the young woman sobbed."

Being honest, Soaring Eagle gently answered his oldest daughter. "No, Little Deer, I have not. I do not know where they are. I believe the uprising has been subdued. They were with Menawa and the Oakfuskee have had no word of him." Hoping to give his daughter encouragement, he continued, "Horse Stealer and the others may appear any day now."

"How will my father find us?" Blue Bird asked innocently.

"Get'em up and get'em moving," shouted Pete. "Next stop is the pen at Pole Cat Springs."

Chapter Thirty-Five
Time to Go

The Hillabee, the Oakfuskee and the few other families picked up from little towns along the way, all stared in horror at what stood in front of them. Once an agency intended to assist the Creek, now Pole Cat Springs was a stockaded fortress used to hold them in. The summer sun was hot on the people who had walked many, many miles with bad food and very little sleep. They needed desperately to rest.

Several soldiers with shinny new muskets on their shoulders, walked back and forth along the unopened gate. Two more with yellow stripes on their sleeves sat at a table under a scrawny oak tree.

The soldiers were intently looking at a long piece of soiled paper. The names of hundreds of Creek were scribbled there. These would be the next to go.

"Hey Sergeant," Pete yelled out, with no respect for the soldiers. "Got 'ya some more injuns to put in yer pen."

Frowning at the man, the sergeant curtly asked, "Where are they from?"

"Hillabee and Oakfuskee and a few more picked up along the way," Pete answered loudly. "Speck they hungry. Ain't had much to feed' um. You the one got my pay? Think I'll be goin on home now."

"Your payment may be picked up over there," the sergeant said, pointing to a neat log structure. "Thank you for you service," the sergeant added, dismissing the disgusting man.

Looking up at the pitiful group who stood in front of him, the sergeant felt a knot again in his stomach. He was sorry for these poor creatures who had no home and knew not what misfortune lay ahead for them. As he scanned the crowd, he noticed one particular family who seemed different from the others. The man, obviously someone important walked toward him.

"I am Soaring Eagle. I am," he paused, a look of despair covering his face. "I was chief of the Hillabee."

Having heard of the great heroics of the Hillabee Chieftain, the sergeant wondered if this was the same person and decided it was. He stood and almost extended his hand but thought better of it. "Soaring Eagle, I have heard of you. I am surprised that you were brought here," the sergeant said with genuine sorrow in his voice.

Soaring Eagle nodded. "We thought we were being taken to Tuckabatchee. The daughter of Chief Opothle Yahola is the wife of my son. He and other members of my family made the journey with Menawa to help calm the uprising. They have not yet returned," the Hillabee Chieftain said quickly, hoping that this man could help in some way.

Looking down the long list of names on his paper, the sergeant then replied, "Yes, you and your family were supposed to have been taken directly to Tuckabatchee," he frowned, "according to my orders, I will have to place you inside with the others for now," he informed, looking over his shoulder at the stockade. "You will be given food and water," looking at the forlorn face of the once valiant warrior he continued, "I will send one of my privates over to Tuckabatchee to tell Chief Opothle Yahola you are here. If he will sign a note from me and send it back, I will release you to go," the sergeant smiled, "if you give your word of honor that you will go to Tuckabatchee."

Soaring Eagle breathed a sigh of relief. "Where else could we go? Thank you. Is there any chance that I can take all of the Hillabee with me?" Soaring Eagle asked.

"I do not know about that. I will ask my superior officer and Chief Opothle Yahola. How many Hillabee are there?" The sergeant asked.

"Twenty-five counting my family," Soaring Eagle replied.

"Can't make any promises. Come, Soaring Eagle, gather your people. I have to place you inside now," the sergeant instructed, walking over to open the gate. 'Hopefully, you will not remain here long."

Soaring Eagle beckoned his people to move forward and follow him and his family. The gate opened to reveal a large mass of Creek people, many talking among themselves while others sat in silence. Several women had been given the responsibility of keeping the sofkee pot full and the fire burning. Most had been inside the stockade for several days and had become restless and were ready to go…somewhere. These Creek were from several towns scattered along the Tallapoosa and would be moved to the Alabama River. Then be placed on a boat much larger than they could ever imagine, to continue their journey on an even larger boat to an unknown destination. The group was scheduled to leave on that destination in two suns.

Soaring Eagle was greeted by several warriors who made room for the new arrivals. Conversations were subdued and serious. All the people in the stockade seemed to have lost their spirit, even the children sat quietly. The Hillabee Chieftain attempted to offer encouragement and reminded them of the spirit of the grandfathers. The spirit that had guided the Creek people since ancient times.

Soaring Eagle and his fatigued family were fed and then rested as well as possible. With the new sun, a runner from Tuckabatchee arrived at Pole Cat Springs with a signed note from Chief Opothle Yahola. He wanted Soaring Eagle, his family and all the Hillabee released from the stockade. They would leave their homeland with him.

Soaring Eagle bid farewell to his friends and led the Hillabee back to Tuckabatchee. Opothle Yahola welcomed them and the two families were happily reunited. More good news was shared when Opothle Yahola told them he had received word from Menawa. Badger, Horse Stealer and Fox Slayer were unharmed and were returning to Tuckabatchee.

For the first time in many suns, Soaring Eagle saw joy in the faces of his wife and daughter. All his family was safe and would be together when the time came for them to leave.

Opothle Yahola had refrained from telling them that the time would be very soon. He had just met the day before with General Jessup across the river at Talisi. The time was up for the Tuckabatchee people he had said, and they should prepare to leave. When the men returned, they would begin their exodus to their new home in Indian Territory.

Soaring Eagle and his family were sitting quietly by the fire, each one in deep thought about what the future would bring for them. Blue Bird was the first to see the returning men. Jumping up she screamed, "My father, my father."

Horse Stealer was followed by Fox Slayer and Badger. The excited family were both crying and laughing at the same time. Hugs were exchanged, and words of endearment were proclaimed. Laughing, Fox Slayer announced that he must find his wife and son so that all his family would be together.

After the warriors had eaten and the family had composed themselves, Soaring Eagle asked them to join him at the river. Little Flower, Little Deer and Horse Stealer with their children, Blue Bird and Coyote along with Fox Slayer and Little Dove, holding their son, then Morning Star and finally Badger bringing up the rear followed Soaring Eagle to a grassy area that overlooked the Tallapoosa. The beautiful slow-moving river seemed to have a calming effect on any who were troubled.

Soaring Eagle smiled as his family all sat down in front of him. "My family, my beautiful Little Flower and my children and your families and Badger, my great friend and brother," trying not to become emotional, Soaring Eagle paused, clearing his throat. "What times that we have been through, both the good and the bad. Thanks to Sun Flower Woman we had the strength to carry on. She has walked the path to the Giver of Breath, but her spirit will guide us. With the new sun, we will leave this town. It is not our Hillabee home, but is the home of our people. Never again will we see our town of Hillabee. We are strong, and we will face the trials and sorrow that lie ahead. I know that our family and our people will survive," he finished as tears streamed down each face.

"My father and my family," Morning Star added, as she pulled the doll, the stone and the crystal from her pouch. "My doll shows me that we will accept the way of the white people. My crystal shows our path will be hard and sorrowful. The owl's eerie cry will warn of us these difficult times, and my stone will give us strength and courage. As my father has said, we will survive, and we will again be happy."

****

Rays of light danced on the smooth glassy water as the sun rose over the east bank of the Tallapoosa. The early morning quiet was filled with the cheerful song of the red bird, the mockingbird and the sorrowful cry of the morning dove. The sweet smell of late summer filled the air. This day in early September in the year 1836 would be remembered as the end of a way of life for the Tuckabatchee and the family from Hillabee. This would be the day which had long been dreaded and feared. This was the day of departure from the homeland of the grandfathers. Opothle Yahola would gather his people when they had finished the last meal they would ever have here in their town on the banks of the Tallapoosa and then they would go. He had spoken eloquently as he had delivered his last speech the night before in a town where hundreds of talks had been listened to by red men since the ancient times of the grandfathers. The Tuckabatchee people had gathered around the old bent and broken oak tree where Tecumseh had predicted the demise of the Creek Nation and of all the native people. It was here that treaties had been signed that would give to the white man this land. The countless fires of Tuckabatchee had given the old town life. Now, this life would slowly die with the absence of its people. The spirit of these people would never die but would continue to burn brightly for future generations of Creek people.

Chapter Thirty-Six
I Feel It
August 2017

The sun had sunken low in the western sky and no fish had been caught, in fact, the rods were still in the holders on the side of the boat. Matthew looked at Jacob and smiled, "Well buddy, that's my story. Sorry about the fishing. I guess I got a little carried away telling you about my people. Time does seem to slip away down here on the river."

"I don't care about any fish, Matthew," Jacob said. "That was the most amazing story I have ever heard. Do you know what happened when Soaring Eagle and his family left?"

"I was hoping you would ask," Matthew answered happily. "Just as Morning Star had predicted, the journey was hard and sorrowful. The Creek and Cherokee call it, "The Trail Where We Cried." Pausing and looking up at the sky, Matthew untied the rope from a Cyprus stump and pushed the boat out and started the motor.

"There is more, right?" Jacob asked. "We aren't leaving are we. I do not want to go yet."

Matthew laughed, "No, we aren't leaving yet, but we will have to soon. Don't need to be down here at night. I am just moving to a different place to finish."

"Why?" Jacob asked, confused.

"You'll understand," Matthew replied, "I will finish the story in a few minutes."

Matthew quickly guided the little boat upriver. The air blowing in their faces, sweet and cool. Finding the spot on the river bank he was looking for; the young man expertly pulled the boat into a little slew. "O.K.," pulling two Cokes from the ice chest and handing one to Jacob, "I'll finish now. Chief Opothle Yahola's Tuckabatchee and the Hillabee family were

Just A Cotton Field

led overland all the way to Indian Territory. Some of them had horses and there were a few wagons, but most walked." Other groups of Creek traveled overland part of the way and then were placed on boats to finish their journey."

"Did all of the Creek go to Indian Territory?" Jacob questioned, when Matthew paused.

"No, actually some went north and lived among the Cherokee, but in a year or two, the Cherokee were forced to go too. Some of the Creek women married white men and they were allowed to stay. A few of them were smart enough to hold on to their land allotment and accepted the white man's laws. This didn't last too long in most cases. The dishonest white man usually found a way to take the land. And then there were the few who hid out in the woods," Matthew laughed. "I think they were the smartest."

"Did they manage to stay here?" Jacob asked, taking a drink of his Coke.

"Yeah, for the most part. And, you know what? Some of them accidently," Matthew laughed again, "got lost in the woods while looking for food and came back to these lands. A few more made the entire trip to Indian Territory, but also found a way back. Many people here today are descendants of these groups."

"Are you?" Jacob excitedly asked.

"Maybe," Matthew said smiling.

"Hey, what happened to old Chief Menawa?" Jacob inquired.

"That's sad too," Matthew said, touching his nose. "Think I got a little too much sun," looking at his friend, he added, "and so have you. Well, remember Menawa was the leader at the Horseshoe and he somehow managed to survive. After the Creek War, the old chief settled down again at his old town of Oakfuskee. Then later, was sent to enforce the death penalty at Acorn Bluff. When the uprising of 1836 began, the government asked him to help calm the insurgents down. 'Course you know that Badger, Fox Slayer and Horse Stealer went too.

He was promised that he and his family would be allowed to stay here. In some sort of a mix up, or maybe trickery, he was forced to go just like everybody else. I remember reading that he was asked and was given permission to spend one last night at his Oakfuskee Town. The next day he told a white man, "Last evening I saw the sun set for the last time, and its light shine upon the treetops, the land and the water, that I am never to look upon again."

"So, what happened to him?" Jacob asked hesitantly.

"He died somewhere on the journey. He was buried in an unmarked grave. No one knows where," Matthew said softly as he looked at the setting sun. "Need to finish up pretty quickly."

"O.K.," Jacob answered. "Now tell me what happened to Soaring Eagle and his family. Did they make it all the way to Indian Territory?"

"Yes, they actually faired better than many of the Creek. Leaving in the late summer, they did not have to deal with the cold. Many, in other groups, actually froze to death. They were often hungry, not having enough food, then lying down on their blankets with only stars to cover them. Many, many of the oldest and the youngest did not have the strength to survive. To use the words of Soaring Eagle, they walked the path to the Great Spirit. And just as Menawa, were buried in unmarked graves along the way." With a slight crack in his voice, Matthew continued. "Jacob, thousands of these people died. Nearly a quarter of the entire Cherokee Nation and almost that many Creek, and for what? Just so some white man could take their land and steal their home." Matthew said breathlessly. "Sorry, buddy, this just makes me so mad. That's pretty much it for the day. We need to go."

"There is more, isn't there?" Jacob asked.

Matthew nodded, "Yes, but that's another story for another day," he said, reaching to start the outboard motor again.

"Wait," Jacob demanded. "What about Morning Star, she wasn't a witch was she? What happened to her?"

"I'm glad you asked, Jacob," Matthew smiled, "she was definitely not a witch. In fact, it was the strength and courage she received from Sun Flower Woman and the grandmothers that helped her family survive the hardships they faced."

"Sure, would like to have met her," Jacob proclaimed as he gingerly touched his sunburned nose.

"Me too, buddy, me too," Matthew softly said, "I would have loved to have known my great, great grandmother."

"Man, oh man, Jacob exclaimed as both brushed the moisture from their eyes. "Now, tell me why we came to this spot for you to finish the story."

Smiling Matthew slowly said, "On the other side of those bushes is the old town of Tuckabatchee. Remember, that was the home of Opothle Yahola and some of Soaring Eagle's family, my people. When they were forced to leave, it has been said that they turned and looked one final time at the sun as it rose over the east bank of the Tallapoosa."

Shadows had begun to fall as Matthew maneuvered the boat onto the old trailer. The two young men stood in silence, both thinking of what had been in the distant past. Taking one final look at the timeless flow of the river, Matthew and Jacob climbed into the truck.

"I think we have just enough time to feel," Matthew began and then stopped.

"Feel what?" Jacob asked curiously.

Matthew smiled again, "I think you will know without me telling you." He slowly guided the old truck along the rut-filled road, coming to a complete stop at the top of the rise. He turned the engine off and got out of the truck. Jacob did the same. The sound of the fading day, sounds the Creek people had heard, the far-off call of the dove and the final song of the redbird broke the silence. The earthy smell of the cotton filled the air. Then it happened, the call of the owl, sad and melancholy.

Jacob looked at Matthew, "I feel it," he said. "I feel the spirit of your people. They are still here. Oh, my Gosh, they are really here." Jacob looked out at the vast cotton field in front of him. "This was their home. It is not, Just A Cotton Field."

The End

Epilogue

Obviously, I have a deep passion for anything Native American, especially for the people who roamed the banks of the Tallapoosa River. I also love the Tallapoosa; the beauty of the river is unmatched, and the peaceful serenity is soothing. The river seems to have captured and continues to hold something special from the long-ago past. For me, this is the spirit of the people who made their homes along the river. After reading *Just A Cotton Field*, I hope that you too can experience that feeling. I promise that spirit really does exist, if one truly wants to find it.

Glossary of Creek Words
And
Meanings of Towns, Place Names, Creeks and Rivers

Culuffadee – White Oak Creek, current name is Harbuck Creek, probable site of the Creek Mother Town of Hillabee

Hillabee – Swift or Quick, likely referring to the flow of water, resulting in the name of the village

Lockchau Talofa – Acorn Bluff, Home of William McIntosh

Tallapoosa – (Early name, Oakfuskee/Fawn) Rock pulverized, little rocks, also cat in the cane break

Chattahoochee – Marked or Flowered Rocks

Saugahatchee – Turtle Rattle Creek

Oakfuskee – Point Between Streams

Tuckabatchee – Incorrect Town, one not sufficiently strick, Is-po-co-gee, ancient name meaning Town of Survivors

Coweta – Vague ancient word having to do with eastward migration or meaning "to go"

Huti – Creek House

Bear Grass – Passv or Button Snakeroot, used as medicine to reduce fever and heal sickness

Sofkee – Mush or Soup made from corn

Just A Cotton Field

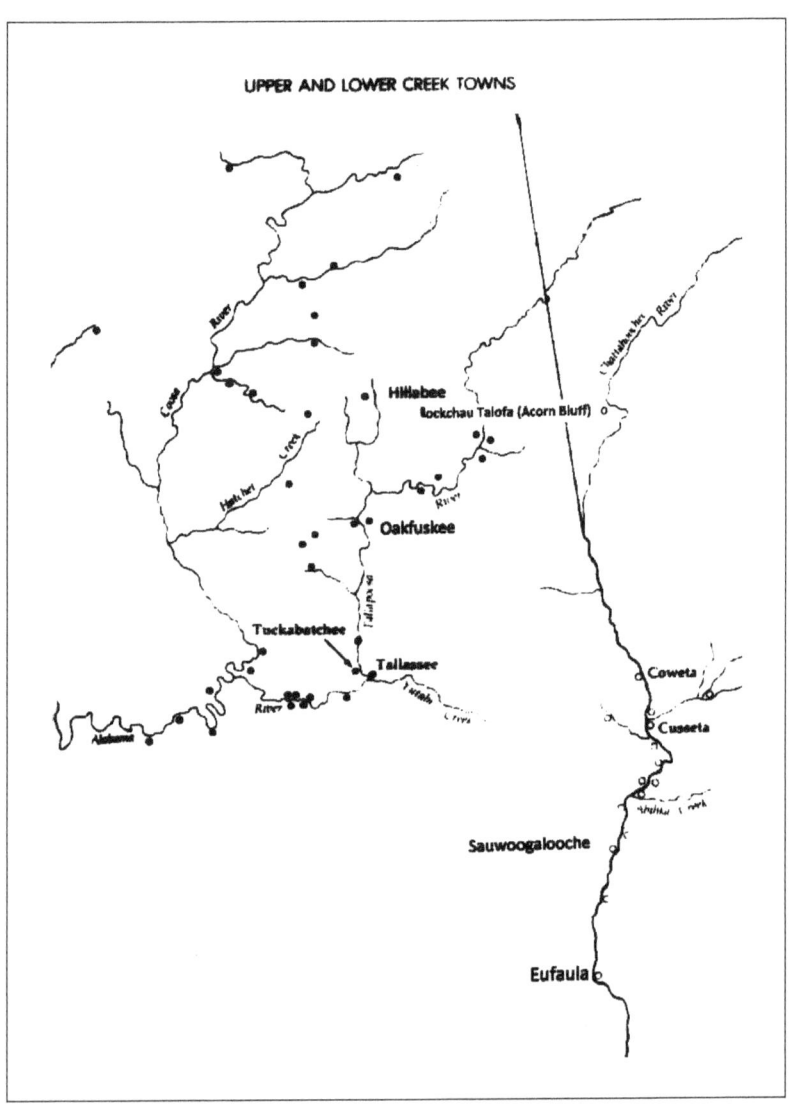

Map of Upper and Lower Creek Towns.

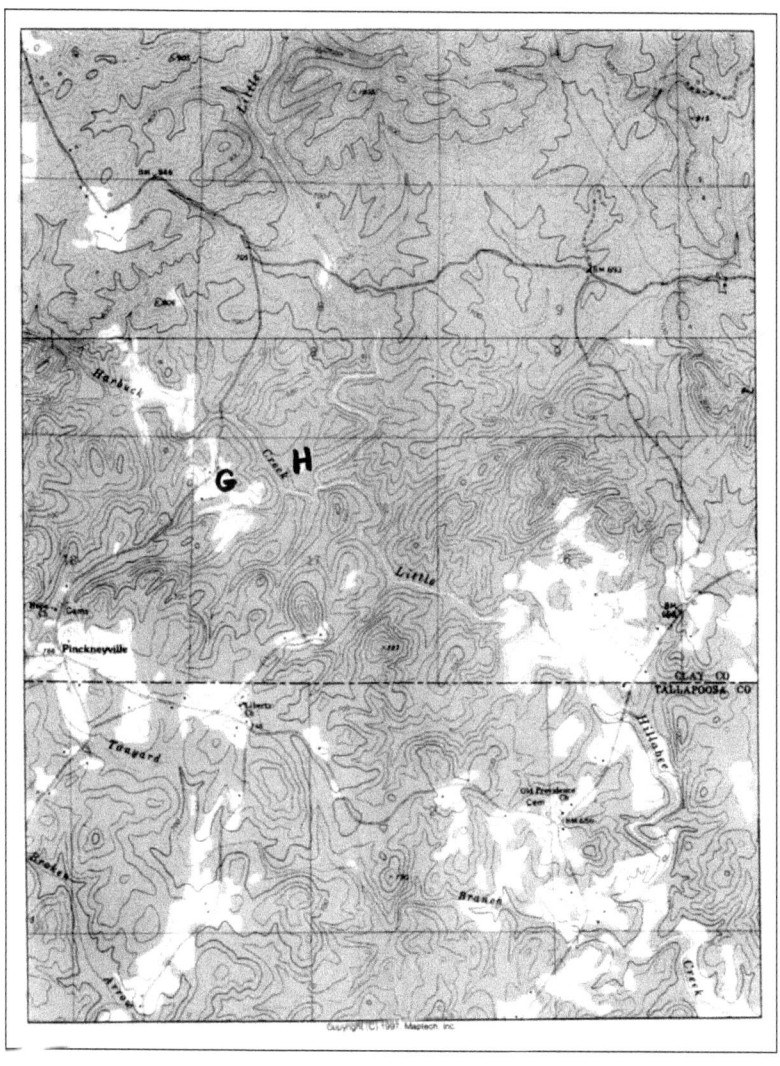

Topo Map of Hillabee Village and Grierson Farm Sites.

Culuffadee or White Oak Creek, present day Harbuck Creek.

Historical Marker at McIntosh Reserve.

Council Bluffs Treaty Marker.

Chief William McIntosh Story.

Replica of McIntosh Cabin at Acorn Bluff.

Acorn Bluff Inn and Tavern.

Author Debra Hughey at Acorn Bluff.

Gravesite of William McIntosh at Acorn Bluff.

Chattahoochee River at Acorn Bluff.

Chattahoochee River at McIntosh Reserve, Whitesburg, Georgia.

Moore-Davis Nursery at Site of Pole Cat Springs on U.S. Highway 80 in Macon County, Alabama.

The Author Debra Hughey with Property Owner Webb Davis Overlooking the Pole Cat Springs site. Today the Site is an Overgrown Ravine.

Tuckabatchee Old Field Site. Today, *Just A Cotton Field* ... The Beginning, May It Never End.

Debra Hughey

Dirt Road Winds Through Tuckabatchee Cotton Field.

Tuckabatchee Boat Ramp at Taylor Farm's on the Tallapoosa River.

— More Books By Debra Hughey —

People of the Townhouse..$19.95

Debra Hughey is considered by many as the expert of Creek Indian culture and history in the Tallapoosa River Valley of East-Central, Alabama. Discovering new things about the original inhabitants of Tallassee, Alabama, has been her life-long passion.

The Owl and The Horseshoe..$14.95

Debra Hughey chronicles the typical Creek village prior to the decisive Battle of Horseshoe Bend in 1814, providing the reader with an intimate capsule of Creek life in the Hillabee Village of central Alabama.

Spirit of the Red Stick Women $14.95

Debra Hughey tells of the aftermath of General Andrew Jackson's 1814 victory over the Red Stick Warriors at the Battle of Horseshoe Bend which ended Creek Indian dominance in Alabama. Approximately, 1,000 Creek men were killed at the Horseshoe, leaving a few old men and the Creek women and children refugees in their own country. Debra Hughey's story of the plight of the widows and orphans of the massacred Red Stick Warriors is one which has likely never been told.

www.ingramcontent.com/pod-product-compliance
Lightning Source LLC
Chambersburg PA
CBHW052132110526
44591CB00012B/1693